Building an Award-Winning
Guitar Program

Building an Award-Winning Guitar Program

A Guide for Music Educators

BILL SWICK

OXFORD
UNIVERSITY PRESS

OXFORD
UNIVERSITY PRESS

Oxford University Press is a department of the University of Oxford. It furthers
the University's objective of excellence in research, scholarship, and education
by publishing worldwide. Oxford is a registered trade mark of Oxford University
Press in the UK and certain other countries.

Published in the United States of America by Oxford University Press
198 Madison Avenue, New York, NY 10016, United States of America.

Library of Congress Cataloging-in-Publication Data
Names: Swick, Bill, author.
Title: Building an award-winning guitar program: a guide for music educators / Bill Swick.
Description: New York : Oxford University Press, 2022. | Includes index.
Identifiers: LCCN 2022010866 (print) | LCCN 2022010867 (ebook) |
ISBN 9780197609804 (hardback) | ISBN 9780197609811 (paperback) |
ISBN 9780197609835 (epub)
Subjects: LCSH: Guitar teachers—Vocational guidance. |
Music teachers—Vocational guidance. | Guitar—Instruction and study—
Vocational guidance. | Music—Instruction and study—Vocational guidance.
Classification: LCC ML3795 .S925 2022 (print) | LCC ML3795 (ebook) |
DDC 780.23—dc23/eng/20220303
LC record available at https://lccn.loc.gov/2022010866
LC ebook record available at https://lccn.loc.gov/2022010867

DOI: 10.1093/oso/9780197609804.001.0001

1 3 5 7 9 8 6 4 2

Paperback printed by Lakeside Book Company, United States of America
Hardback printed by Bridgeport National Bindery, Inc., United States of America

Contents

1

Guitar and the Rise
of "Innovative" Ensembles

It was 2005, and I was sitting in a large ballroom with over a thousand other music educators in the convention center for the Music Educators National Conference in Minneapolis, Minnesota, when we were told that music education was in crisis. Student enrollment in music classes such as band, choir, and orchestra was dropping at an alarming rate nationwide. Music educators were going to lose their jobs if they could not figure out ways to attract students to their classrooms. The message was clear: we needed to start considering all types of alternatives, such as guitar, music technology, mariachi, bluegrass, rock band, song writing, music theory, handbells—any type of music class that would attract students and save jobs.

The overall mood of the conference that year was quite grim. It was serious. The presenters had charts, diagrams, and the hard facts to show that the traditional music classes were no longer as attractive to students as they once had been. Everything suggested that a change was coming. School music education had to transform itself in order to survive.

Interestingly, that same year, a popular video game called Guitar Hero was released in November, just in time for the holiday season. The controller for the game was a small, plastic version of a guitar.

Understanding Guitar Education in the United States

The years 2006 through 2010, following that grim Music Educators National Conference, there showed a particularly high interest among students in joining guitar classes (a trend that may have linked directly to the popularity of Guitar Hero). Schools began to respond. With decreased enrollment in more traditional music classes, many band directors no longer had six classes of band, but maybe three classes of band, one class of jazz band, and two classes of music appreciation or other music-related fillers. During this peak

Building an Award-Winning Guitar Program. Bill Swick, Oxford University Press. © Oxford University Press 2022.
DOI: 10.1093/oso/9780197609804.003.0001

of student interest in the guitar, administrators quickly learned that they could easily fill guitar classes, which became increasingly common. In some schools, band, choir, and even orchestra teachers were given guitar classes to teach to fill their schedules.

Of course, some states have been more inviting than others in terms of accepting guitar into the classroom. Region seems to play a factor. For instance, numbers suggest that states below the 40N latitude seem to be more hospitable to guitar than states north of that line.[1] Similarly, related programs like mariachi have tended to develop in only a small region of the country, in states like Arizona, Nevada, California, New Mexico, and Texas. Programs like bluegrass are developing in the eastern region of the United States. Rock band, on the other hand, is sporadic nationwide.

Overall, however, guitar classes were doubtlessly growing in popularity. This transition has affected how universities prepare their music education majors to become future teachers. The results of two independent surveys indicate that current music education students have an 80 to 90 percent chance of teaching one or more classes of guitar once the educators have entered the teaching field, though much depends on the area of the country where the educators live and plan to teach.[2] Some universities have even made changes in their curriculum to include a semester of guitar pedagogy to better prepare future music students for the changing times.

What is covered under the category of "guitar pedagogy" is evolving as well. Some guitar classes have begun including ukulele, and others have also added banjo and/or mandolin. Even though there are national standards for teaching guitar, the newness of these alternative ensembles means that there are currently no clear guidelines for what is acceptable and what is not for a guitar class or ensemble. The idea at this moment is to attract students into the classroom and hold their interest. If programs are well attended, they are likely to be kept. Classes with low attendance are likely to be replaced with something more popular.

The rise in popularity of guitar classes, however, has not been without challenges. Even as universities begin to include guitar pedagogy for music education majors, the number of guitar teachers has not met the growing demand. When schools began to offer guitar classes taught by band, choir, or even orchestra teachers, the reality was that these music teachers often did not play the guitar, and many had no interest in learning.

The challenges that mismatch causes can be seen through a case study of my own school district: Clark County School District in Las Vegas, Nevada.

In 1996, the district, the fifth largest school district in the United States, started its first guitar program in one middle school. Fifteen years later, Clark County offered guitar classes in a total of sixty-two schools with approximately 5,700 guitar students enrolled. During this time, few colleges were offering a music education degree with an emphasis in guitar, so finding qualified, licensed guitar teachers was a major challenge. Of the sixty-two music educators teaching guitar in the Clark County School District in 2011, only twelve had majored in guitar during college. The other fifty music educators had majored in areas related to band, choir, and orchestra. Many from this group had never played a guitar prior to teaching it.

The growth of guitar classes in Clark County was so explosive that most decisions were made by trial and error, and there were inevitably mistakes along the way. For years, Clark County experienced a 30 percent annual turnover of music educators who were teaching guitar as a secondary instrument. Music educators were demonstrating that they would rather change or quit their jobs than teach guitar. At some point, school principals even began to eliminate guitar classes to retain their music teachers. To tackle this turnover issue, Clark County became more aggressive in offering regular professional development classes on how to teach guitar, providing weekly lesson plans for the teachers along with supplementary teaching materials for those non-guitar-playing music educators.

The lesson learned from Clark County is clear: when assigning music educators to teach alternative music classes like guitar, school administrators must provide plenty of supportive professional development, a mentoring program for teachers, and a supply of weekly classroom materials to assist teachers in succeeding in teaching in an area in which they are not familiar. Today, Clark County offers guitar classes in forty schools and now has stable teacher retention. Though this stability is partly because Clark County has been able to hire more teachers who majored in guitar at college, a number of music educators who started off as band directors have also found they prefer teaching guitar full time, as opposed to teaching band part time, showing the success of a strong professional development and support system.

Other challenges exist for guitar programs in the United States. Music programs such as band, choir, and orchestra have been in public schools since about 1920. During this time, many structures have been established to maintain these programs to make certain they are financially supported and continue to attract students. Almost every university music school has a band, a choir, and an orchestra, and learning to teach and direct these ensembles has been the focus of music education since about 1940. Though there are some indicators that this trend is slowly changing, by comparison, little is being done at the university level to prepare future music educators to lead and develop alternative ensembles.

Band, choir, and orchestra also have the benefit of widespread music-education-association support. Almost every state in the union has a state chapter of the Music Educators Association, which is part of the National Association for Music Education (NAfME). These organizations often sponsor solo and ensemble festivals as well as honor ensembles at the local, regional, and state levels. For the most part, however, these events are available only to students who participate in band, choir, or orchestra—although a handful of states are now accepting guitar into some of these events by including an all-state guitar ensemble.

In 2018, NAfME created the very first All-National Honor Guitar Ensemble. National honor ensembles have been in place for band, choir, and orchestra for decades. Adding guitar was a big historic step for guitar education in the United States and for promotion of guitar education in US schools. The following year, in 2019, NAfME added the first All-National Honor Rock Band. This too was a historic move not just for guitar, but also for promotion of commercial/popular music as an acceptable form of music education in schools. NAfME also plans to add mariachi into the All-National Honor Ensembles.

Though the opportunities for guitar students are starting to look a little more like the opportunities for music students in band, choir, and orchestra, this is still true only in fewer than half of the states. The other half of the states are still concerned that if guitar is offered in school, all of the band students are going to drop band and join the guitar class. When we look at the states that have included guitar, no evidence supports this fear, which nevertheless persists for states that have not yet tried it.

In the Clark County School District, for example, we kept close records of the number of students who left band, choir, and orchestra classes to join a guitar class. Some upper classmen have enough elective choices to attend both band and guitar, a decision that has no effect on either class. These students were not counted as leaving one class for another. Over a period of twenty years in Clark County, the total number of students dropping band, choir, or orchestra to join a guitar class was minimal—fewer than two or three students a year! And when following up on these cases, we found that students dropped band mostly at the encouragement of the band director and joined a guitar class to fill the elective time. In these cases, the band directors were thrilled to remove these often dissatisfied students from their classes and were happy they had somewhere else to go. Guitar classes proved to be a win/win for all involved.

Why and How to Use This Book

Since 2005, alternative ensembles have developed in various parts of the country. Many states require high school students to earn a minimum of one fine arts credit as a requirement for graduation, and for students looking for just one year of study in music, band and orchestra are not necessarily the answer. Classes like guitar, handbells, rock band, and music technology have provided an alternative to traditional music appreciation classes and may prove to be more attractive to students with additional elective credits to fill.

These alternative ensembles were soon renamed "innovations," because some of the leaders in alternative ensembles felt the word "alternative" sounded negative. In 2011 NAfME created the first Innovations Council, made up of music educators who represent these types of ensembles. The role of the council is to advocate for equality for the students who participate in these "innovative" groups.

There have been many benefits to music education as a result of these innovative ensembles. One argument is that students who took these classes left high school more musically well rounded. For example, choir students were able to take guitar and learn to accompany themselves singing. Band students were able to study music technology and expand their musical knowledge by using music apps and software. Choir students took handbells and learned to read music and count rhythms, or enhance the reading and counting skills they already had. Orchestra students were able to take rock band and find new ways to express their musical interest. The addition of innovations not only secured employment for music educators (disproving band, choir, and orchestra teachers' arguments that adding innovative ensembles would result in students leaving band, choir, and orchestra to join the more attractive alternative groups), but it also provided an opportunity to widen the musical experience for students.

Of all of these innovations, guitar ensembles or guitar classes have taken the lead in terms of student enrollment. At a recent NAfME conference, the enrollment numbers for guitar nationwide were just under the total national enrollment for orchestra. There is a clear need for greater resources, not just to help guitar teachers actually teach guitar, but also to help them better serve and advocate for their students and programs.

I wrote this book to share my many years of experience as a guitar teacher leading an award-winning program and to help other music teachers build their own school guitar programs. However, much of the advice I give in the following chapters apply to all innovative music classes. Some topics are guitar specific, yet much of the content of this book could apply to any of the other innovative classes we are seeing develop across the country. As you read this book, the word "guitar" may be interchanged with any alternative class or ensemble that you may be teaching. The principles are the same.

This book is divided into chapters that cover individual areas important to building an award-winning program. The aim of this book is to help music teachers pave a path for all students interested in music to have the same opportunities as all other students, regardless of the music classes in which they are enrolled. A student's choice of instrument should not come with limitations, and all students should have the same possibilities and opportunities as the next. At the time of this writing, this is not the case. Yet if directors of innovative ensembles follow the guidelines outlined in this text, the situation will improve, and more opportunities will appear. It is up to all of us, as music educators, to take steps to provide equal opportunities for all of our music students.

Qualities of an Effective Music Educator

Seldom do music educators consciously think about building an award-winning music program. Those who accomplish this feat are generally focused, are driven, and tend to excel in the areas in which they are interested. But before we dive into evaluating guitar programs that are considered award winning, let's look at some other organizations that have been around in schools for much longer. For example, what does it take to build an award-winning band program, or orchestra program, or choir or theater program? What are some of the key elements necessary to create programs that catch the attention of other music educators?

In his book, *Introduction to Effective Music Teaching: Artistry and Attitude,* Alfred S. Townsend describes effective music educators as teachers who place the needs of the organization above their own. A good music teacher is an effective collaborator and communicator. An effective music education requires conciliation and a commitment to the growth of the whole student. The effective teacher sets and achieves significant goals.

Townsend writes that he once saw the following statement on the desk of a coach, "There is no limit to how far we can go if it doesn't matter who gets the credit."[3]

Townsend also suggests that effective educators know and readily use all students' names and birthdays. One method that many music educators have adopted is to create a seating chart the very first week of school and ask each student about their preferred names. The director should keep this seating chart available during each class and make a point of calling each student by their preferred name. Within a few weeks, you will know every student's name.

With most online grading software, student birthdays are readily available. During the first week of school, print a monthly calendar for the year and write in the birthdays of each of your students. Doing so will take a little effort and time, but once it is done, it will be done for the school year. Being able to recognize each of your students on their birthday will go a long way, particularly if you mention their birthday without being reminded.

At this point, you may be comparing yourself to Townsend's descriptions of an effective music teacher and doing a self-evaluation. In your effort to become more effective, just know there are many perceptions and opinions of what makes a good teacher. Here are real titles of articles found online by doing a simple Google search with "qualities of a music educator":

"Music Teacher Qualities That Students Look For"[4]
"10 Qualities of a Great Music Teacher"[5]
"The Top 8 Qualities to Look for in a Great Music Teacher"[6]
"7 Important Characteristics of an Excellent Music Teacher"[7]
"10 Essential Characteristics of Successful Music Instructors"[8]
"What Makes a Great Music Teacher?"[9]
"Qualities of a Great Music Teacher"[10]
"7 Essential Qualities Every Music Teacher Should Have"[11]
"19 Things That Great Music Teachers Do"[12]

Collectively found in the previous articles are over eighty outstanding qualities that others perceive an effective music educator should possess. That is a lot of boxes to check. Fortunately, there is some duplication, but even with the duplications, there are many skills and qualities associated with an effective music educator. Most music educators are not going to have all of the qualities listed. But this list may be considered a good resource for considering how others perceive the abilities of an effective music educator.

Effective Music Educator Self-Reflection Quiz

In an effort to break this down, the following worksheet has been created and lists the top twenty qualities found in these individual lists. Before jumping into the contents of this book, take some time to self-reflect and take the quiz. What are the qualities that you think you demonstrate, and what are qualities that you think you need to work on? Each statement has been written as an affirmation, starting with the word "I" followed by a description. As you read each statement, make a note if you agree or disagree. Four *N*s is equivalent to an 80 percent. Two *N*s is equivalent to a 90 percent and so on. Getting 100 percent is not as important as it is to become aware of the qualities you recognize within yourself and the ones that you may need to work on. This quiz may be found in Appendix A: "Qualities of an Effective Music Educator."

2

Building an Infrastructure for Success

American author John Maxwell is often quoted as saying, "It takes a team to build a dream." A version of this quotation then became the title of his 2002 book, *Teamwork Makes the Dream Work*. The basic idea is it takes a great many people to create something big and special. The complete quotation by Maxwell reads, "Teamwork makes the dream work, but a vision becomes a nightmare when the leader has a big dream and a bad team."[1] His statement is the focus of this chapter. Building an award-winning music program cannot be done by just one person. It makes no difference how knowledgeable a music educator may be about teaching music; building something outstanding requires a team, and each team member must contribute toward excellence in order to experience the dream.

Many educators believe that programs are successful because the students in a particular school or program are so talented. Students come and go, however. Eventually, they all go. An award-winning program cannot be built from the talent of a single class of students. That program must first create the talent once students have arrived, and then maintain it.

Before you as an ensemble leader can start creating that talent, you must have a clear vision of the dream. What is the dream? What defines your goals? How are you going to know when you have reached your dreams? What does an award-winning music program look like to you? Is it even important to you to have an award-winning program, or are you more interested in building a sustainable program that continually attracts and engages your students and teaches them lifelong musical skills and appreciation? If the latter resonates with you, then you are on your way to building an award-winning program! Yet no matter your specific dream, how to get there is not quite as important as it is to know who is going to assist and support you in achieving your goals. Nothing can be accomplished without a strong infrastructure of administrative, faculty, staff, and community support. Who is on your team and how can you all work together? The contents of this chapter are about building the infrastructure for your program from the ground up, starting with your people.

Building an Award-Winning Guitar Program. Bill Swick, Oxford University Press. © Oxford University Press 2022. DOI: 10.1093/oso/9780197609804.003.0002

Who Is on Your Campus?

Once during a new-teacher orientation meeting, someone suggested that the most important person in the school to befriend is the head custodian. I've heard others say that it is the school banker. Then there are those who say it is the person in charge of graphic arts and printing. Each of these statements has a lot of truth in it, and I consider them all solid advice. The reality is that *all* of these people are important, as are many others who contribute to the school.

Start by taking inventory of who is on campus. Make a list of faculty members, administration, and staff members and what their skills are. Many of these people will have skills you may not have or time to do tasks you do not have time to do. Each school is different, but the following list may assist you in making your own list of those on your campus who can assist you in fulfilling your dreams.

Administrators

1. School principal: Every school should have a principal. The question is, does your principal have a musical background? Does the principal play guitar or any other musical instrument? Is the principal supportive of the arts? This information is important to know or find out, because it could make a difference where you find your support.
2. Assistant principal: Most schools have at least one assistant principal or a number of assistant principals, depending on the population of the school. The same questions apply with regard to assistant principal(s) as with the principal. Do any play guitar? Do any play a musical instrument? Again, this information is important.
3. Dean: Most schools have one or more deans. The same questions as in (1) and (2) apply for deans. Deans are likely to chaperone trips or be the administrators on duty for activities such as performances or concerts.

Learning about the administration is important. Chances are that one of these individuals will be your administrative supervisor. It is also important to have a positive relationship with your supervisor, because this person is going to be doing classroom observations, attending concerts, and writing your teacher evaluation.

It is likely that one of these administrators will also be in charge of activities. That is, one of the administrators will be in charge of the calendar, will approve performances on and off campus, will control the content of the school website, and will oversee travel, clubs, publicity, and all student-related activities. Your relationship with this person will make a difference in how much help and support you and your program will receive. It is important to create and maintain a healthy, professional relationship with this person.

One of your administrators will be in charge of facilities, including heating and air conditioning, leaking roofs, plumbing, paint, windows, desks, and furniture. Basically, anything and everything that you need that is a physical object will fall under facilities. For a string teacher, for instance, having the correct temperature and humidity for instrument storage is very important. Having a good relationship with this administrator will play a key role in how well your instruments hold up, particularly during the summer months when the air conditioning is typically turned off in most parts of the campus.

One of your administrators will be in charge of inventory. It will be your responsibility to maintain a spreadsheet of everything that is kept in your room, such as every instrument, including the serial number, the brand, and the year it is added to the inventory. Maintaining this inventory spreadsheet of music, instruments, sound equipment, lighting, electronics, and everything purchased for the music program is of utmost importance. Working with this administrator will be key, because the inventory sheet is an important record for reference when the time comes to replace instruments.

The dean's office will usually be the first stop for students who are unruly and have stepped out of line. It is important that you understand the guidelines for sending a student to the dean's office to be disciplined. Some schools suggest that teachers send students to the dean's office only if weapons, drugs, or blood are involved. Other schools want disruptive students removed from the classrooms. Be sure to familiarize yourself with the expectations of the dean's office. In general, the fewer students you refer to this office, the more you will be appreciated.

Staff

Staff are professionals who work on campus but do not teach. These important people are on campus to assist administrators and teachers to make their jobs a little easier. Staff members will vary from school to school, but I list some common roles here.

1. Secretaries: Most administrators and some faculty members have secretaries, depending on the number of students enrolled in a program. As a general rule, if you do not have an assigned secretary, asking for assistance from someone else's secretary is considered inappropriate.

2. Banker: Most schools have a banker. This person is responsible for all of the money that is collected and spent for the entire school. It can be a stressful job. As mentioned at the beginning of this chapter, making friends with the banker is generally a good idea. Just as importantly, doing all of your accounting paperwork completely and correctly when it comes to money is key—and can go a long way in maintaining a good relationship with your school banker. The banker cuts checks, generally once a week. For those times when you may need a check written immediately, you are basically asking for a favor. Hence it helps to have a friendly relationship with the person in a position to do that favor.

3. Graphic artist/printer: Some schools have a full-time graphic artist and/or printer, the person you would visit for multiple copies of teaching materials. In some cases, this is also the person who creates posters, program covers, or bound books. The graphic artist/printer is also the keeper of colored butcher paper and all copy paper—not only in white, but in a variety of colors as well. In some schools, this person is also the keeper of facial tissues and printer cartridges, as well as postal deliveries that are too big to fit into a teacher's mailbox. The graphic artist/printer is another person on whom you will depend and with whom you will want to maintain a good working relationship.

4. Custodian staff: Almost all schools have a custodian staff that starts early before teachers and students arrive and works late, sometimes well into the night, possibly in two shifts. This is the team of staff members who move furniture, empty waste baskets, clean floors, clean bathrooms, clean the cafeteria, and pick up the grounds, among an extensive list of responsibilities. Needless to say, these staff members are integral to the smooth operations of the school. From time to time, you will need a favor done by one of the custodians. The most common

request is for someone to unlock a door, because this team has keys to the entire campus. It always helps to have a good relationship with everyone on this team.

5. Security staff: This team of staffers may be school police or may be workers who focus on keeping students and faculty safe. They are the first responders. When parents come to school to withdraw their children before the end of the school day, a member of the security staff generally finds those students and escorts them to the school office. The security staff members are always visible any time students are on campus. It always helps to have a good relationship with everyone on this team. Depending on the school, security staff members may be required to be present at all after-school and evening functions. They are often scheduled to remain on duty until the last student has been picked up.

6. Theater manager: Not all schools will have a full-time theater manager, but some schools do. The responsibility of theater manager is sometimes given to a faculty member, usually a theater teacher. The theater manager turns on the lights in the theater, is knowledgeable about the sound system, and knows how to turn on and off everything within the theater. For a music teacher, being familiar with someone in the theater who knows lights, sound, and all of the other details about the facility makes giving performances much easier. Once again, it is good to have a cordial working relationship with the theater manager, particularly if you plan on having performances in the theater.

Staff members are there to provide service when and where service is needed. They may never experience two days alike, because the needs change daily just as the people in need change daily. It is so important to have a good working relationship with everyone on staff. Most people do not contact staffers unless they need something that very minute. To build a good relationship with staff members, make a point to go see them and visit without needing anything at the time. These staff members perform integral tasks at the school that can often go unnoticed or unappreciated by students and faculty alike. Show your appreciation by sharing treats with them. Some staff members like chocolate. Others like cookies. Before offering treats, be sure to inquire about dietary restrictions and follow all school policies related to sharing food with colleagues. Find out what they like and treat them from time to time. Be professional, courteous, and friendly.

Faculty

As you most likely know from your own experiences, your fellow faculty members spend most of their time teaching and do not have a lot of extra time. Start by creating a good relationship with the faculty members in your department. For a music teacher this connection could include the band director, choir teacher, orchestra conductor, mariachi teacher, and jazz band director. In some cases, you may have all of those roles or at least more than one. Even if you are at a school with a small music faculty, there should be other teachers of fine arts, like theater, art, and dance, with whom you can work closely. Collaboration is something that we encourage in our students, and one of the best ways to model collaboration is to work with other faculty members in such a way that students see and experience.

The following are some collaboration ideas with other faculty members.

- English/literature teacher: Coordinate with the literature teacher about which novels students are reading in class. Teach music from the same historical period and cultural context and have students perform music in their literature class as a way to bridge music and literature.
- Dance teacher: Coordinate a musical selection in which dance students may demonstrate a dance from any style of music: for example, dancing to a tango or rhumba. Have dance students dance as music students perform the music.
- Art teacher: Arrange with the art teacher for art students to paint or draw something related to the music being performed at a concert. They may create their artwork on stage during a musical performance, and their art may be seen on the stage as a visual while the audience is listening to music.
- Videography teacher: Arrange to have the teacher or students record musical performances and edit the videos, perhaps in creative ways that build videography skills taught in the class.
- Theater teacher: Arrange for theater students to run the box office, collect tickets, pass out programs, operate lights and sound, and seat guests for concerts. In exchange, you and your students will do the same for them during their performances.
- Choir teacher: Coordinate music that vocalists and instrumental musicians may perform together. Your students can perform as

accompanists during choir concerts and the choir students can perform in your concerts.

- String teacher: Have an exchange with the string teacher that is similar to that with the choir teacher. If you wonder if orchestra students can play along with your students, keep in mind that in the case of guitar classes, you can find arrangements for guitar ensembles and string orchestras, for example.

These are just a few ideas for how to collaborate and teach across the barriers of various types of classes. Your students will see you as someone who is inclusive and desires to work with everyone. That attitude will pass to your students and create a more welcoming environment among all students.

Parents: Creating a Parent Organization

Most schools have a parent-teacher organization or something along those lines. They are sometimes known by other names, but the basic concept is an organization of parents who will have some say in the direction of school procedures and school activities. Though there is usually an existing organization for the entire school, it is not unusual for a band department or choir program to have its own parent organization. Any music program may start its own parent organization.

Some schools call these types of organizations booster clubs, a name that is unfortunately often stigmatized because many assume this term to mean a fundraising organization. Though it is not only possible but also probable that parent organizations raise money, these organizations can do much more in helping you build and advocate for your program.

Part of organizing a parent group requires convincing parents or other kinds of caretakers that they want to belong and be involved. According to Emily Ward in her Music Travel Blog article "Getting Parents Involved in the Music Program," the easiest way to get parents involved in your parent organization is to convince them to join the first year their children attend your school.[2] Jason A. Marshall, Director of Instrumental Music at West Ranch High School, added to Ward's article by writing that

we have tried several things over the year. What works for us is a big push with new parents right at the start of the year. Everything is new for our freshman (parents included) so we go out of our way to try and meet these parents and make them feel welcome. We do a freshman parent social during the first week of band camp where we invite all the new parents, I do a brief introduction, and then some veteran parents explain what our music program is all about. The goal is to not sign anyone up that night, but instead to make them feel welcome and like they are part of the family. We also do a parent performance at the end of our band camp and that is where we start talking to all of our parents about the needs of the program and how they can help. My parent group is amazing and many of the parents socialize together outside of music. This family atmosphere is also a huge recruiting tool for us as the word of mouth alone bring[s] many parents into the fold.[3]

Ward continues, "Before your year even starts, have a marketing campaign ready that is focused on parents. Be resourceful by including information in the school's newsletter. Every parent gets a copy, and it is free advertising. Right out of the gate, it is also a great idea to send letters to the parents of all of the incoming students explaining the music program and invite parents and guardians to a meeting."[4]

How to Get Parents Involved

The following is an excerpt from a question-and-answer page directed to new parents to the Bruton High School Panther Band Booster Organization.[*]

Why Should I Do This? The primary reason for the booster organization is to support your children. The friendships you will make and the enjoyment of participating in the activities are other benefits you will realize. But first and foremost, this is for your child and your child's classmates.

What Can I Do? There are hundreds of things that you can do to be active as a booster. One of the most important things you can do is to attend booster meetings. These meetings are where you should ask questions and voice your concerns and ideas about the organization's activities. This is where the decisions are made, and you should be part of that. Additional ways to help out are to volunteer to chaperone, participate in fund raisers, and/or help out with concerts. Every little thing will make a big difference.

I Am New, Do You Really Need Me? Regardless of your occupation or area of experience, there are many services you would be able to provide to a music program. An important thing to do as a new parent is to get involved right away. Do not wait for someone to ask you to help. Many times, a small nucleus of members does the majority of the work. Parents who are currently in the organization do not know who is willing to volunteer unless you join the organization. New parents are like new students, you are no longer "new" at the end of the school year. Do not wait a year or two to get involved. Time goes by much too quickly.

Why Are They Always Doing Fund Raisers? It takes many thousands of dollars to fund a strong music program. There are instruments, music, sound equipment, travel expenses, and the list goes on and on. Some schools collect a class fee which only covers a small portion of the costs to run a program. If schools allow admission to be charged at performances, that money is also used to run the program. At some point, the costs of running a program will exceed the income of class fees and concert ticket sales. The parent organization will be needed to fund the remaining costs.

* Band Parent Booster Organization Purpose—Bruton High School Panther Band, Sites.Google. com, 2021, https://sites.google.com/site/bhspantherband/band-booster-organization/band-executive-board-purpose.

In today's climate, teachers are constantly expected to do more with less. You may ask, less what? Today's teachers are expected to achieve exceptional results by working with less money, less time, less support, less supervision, and less recognition, just to name a few insufficiencies. A parent organization can help support what the teacher simply cannot do alone. At concert time, if the school employees and student volunteers previously discussed are not available to help, someone will need to design the poster, sell tickets, supervise students, provide snacks between the rehearsal and the concert, design and produce a program, pass out programs, collect tickets, help with promotion, clean up after the performance, clear the stage, assist with sound equipment, assist with video recording, assist with audio recording, supervise the lobby . . . and on and on. One person simply cannot do all these tasks. There must be help, and the most obvious place to start is with parents.

I've been lucky in my experience, in that most parents I've worked with are flattered to be asked to participate in some way and are happy to do most anything. Yet parents are busy, too, and they may not always be free to help. As a general rule, only 20 percent of the total number of parents become volunteers. Eighty percent of my parents never volunteer for anything. However, the 20 percent who do participate are always enough. I've found that some otherwise disengaged parents can be drawn into participating or volunteering if travel is involved. The more exotic the trip, the more parents want to participate; after all, who doesn't like a vacation? Whether these big trips are possible are of course tied to school funding and the general socio-economic status of your student body, but in cases for which this is relevant, you can incentivize parents to participate by requiring that they be members of the booster club for the duration of the entire school year before being eligible to volunteer to take trips.

It was the philosophy of our administration that all students travel and participate despite their ability to pay. During my career, none of my students have been excluded from travel because the lack of money. It is the responsibility of the teacher to know which students cannot afford travel expenses and to seek money from other resources, such as fundraising and the parent booster club. Some schools find ways to fund all travel with no cost to students. Planning ahead makes a big difference. We scheduled an international trip every three years to have time to raise enough money so that all students are able to travel. This is one reason it seems that the school is constantly fundraising.

In preparation for each school year, it is good advice to look back at the previous school year and reflect on how the parent organization assisted with concerts, fundraising, trips, awards night, ensemble festival, and any other events that you may have hosted. Make a list of the areas in which you needed the most help. In that list, describe what skills (if any) are required. For example, ticket sales in my program required parents to attend a training session, be good at operating a computer and printer, and have strong skills at handling money. And of course, they needed to arrive early and stay late. There were not many parents with all of those skills. Selling tickets was the only job for those parents with all of the skills. They were not asked to do anything else.

Some roles require no skills, like collecting tickets, passing out programs, or supervising students backstage. Those positions just need an adult willing to show up and do that job.

Most schools have an open-house night shortly after the school year begins. This is an opportunity for parents to meet their children's teachers, see the classrooms, and experience walking the campus. Open house is an opportunity to distribute information about your parent organization and a listing of volunteer positions with a description of required skills. It is also a good time to have parents sign an attendance sheet and provide an email address and phone number.

Open house is also an opportunity for teachers to meet parents and guardians for the first time. Today, "parents" can mean, for example, two dads, two moms, a single dad, a single mom, an aunt, an uncle, a grandparent, an older sibling, a stepdad, or a stepmom. The traditional mom and dad family also exists. This is a time to encourage all parents and guardians to consider joining the parent booster club and signing up to volunteer from the list of positions you have provided. There is great potential for parents to make new friends and to work together for the betterment of their children's educational experience.

Do Not Be Content to Go Without

Each school will be different and have different resources, but it is important for your vision that you are not content to go without. Always advocate for yourself, your students, and your programs. It is very challenging to build an award-winning music program if the only music your students ever perform is free music that you can find on the Internet, and students are depending on YouTube videos as their source of instruction. Quality programs need quality instruments, fresh strings, music created by world-class composers, method books created by top music educators, and instruction by quality teachers. All this costs money. The education of your students should not be compromised because of the lack of funds.

As a teacher, you will have a supervisory administrator. This will be the administrator with whom you will have the most contact. Do not be shy about expressing the need for any items required to be an effective teacher. If you need instruments, music, method books, strings, music stands, or sound equipment, let your supervisory administrator know. When doing your teacher evaluations, remind your supervisor how much more effective you could be if only your students had the items they needed. Be the squeaky wheel! Do not be content to go without!

If your students' parents can offer support either directly or indirectly, put a parent organization in place and make it clear to your parents that your students are number one to you, and they have needs that must be met to ensure that the best you have to offer is given to their children. Chapter 4 contains some of the many elements of preparing for a performance. Provide the parent booster club with a listing of your "fifteen steps towards a performance" and allow parents to volunteer to assist in the areas in which they feel most comfortable. In addition to discussing how to advocate for funding from the school, Chapter 9 also covers fundraising and other ideas for how to raise money for your program. Make certain your parent organization is an integral part of the fundraising process.

Chances are you will think of other ideas as well. Be aware that each person that you include will be a part of your team to build the program of your dreams. "It takes teamwork to make a dream work."

3

Gaining Recognition

You might imagine that an award-winning music program—especially given the adjective "award-winning"—would have ample plaques, certificates, and trophies on display that share the program's success. While this vision may sound superficial, trophies have a way of saving programs and promoting advocacy. Before dismissing the shallowness of trophies, plaques, and certificates, be mindful that administrators tend not to cancel or discontinue programs that are successful and are actively bringing recognition to the school. During an open-house or other classroom visitation by parents and guests, if the walls of the music room are agleam with glory, the logical assumption is that you have created an award-winning program and parents want their children to be involved. Display your accolades prominently. It is human nature that parents want their children on a winning team and will be proud to share their children's accomplishments to others, and so help to publicize the program within the community.

Yet an award-winning program does not necessarily mean having a room full of trophies and walls filled with plaques and certificates. An award-winning program can have many looks. A trophy is generally an indication that the program has accomplished a certain task. Maybe a program without these visible, tangible emblems of success has not yet participated in events that share recognition of this nature. Maybe there are not yet any events that present trophies for accomplishments in the innovative areas. There are many ways to build recognition beyond just accumulating physical trophies. The purpose of this chapter is to make sure that you and your students are doing everything you can do to enhance the name and reputation of your music program. The following section provides a list of what you can do to bring recognition to your program.

Building an Award-Winning Guitar Program. Bill Swick, Oxford University Press. © Oxford University Press 2022.
DOI: 10.1093/oso/9780197609804.003.0003

Thirty Steps Directors May Take to Bring Recognition to Their Programs

In a secondary music program, students are constantly changing. Building an award-winning program off the backs of specific students for their outstanding talents is possible some years, but not sustainable. Students come and go, but the constant in a program is the director. As a director you can do a great deal to build recognition for yourself and your program. Recognition can come in many forms, but the following list is a good place to start for enhancing your program's reputation. As this reputation grows, the positives will snowball. More and more students and parents will want to be a part of the program, a trend that may lead to more attention from administrators, more funding, more recognition from the community, and more opportunity to keep your program growing.

Find something on this list that appeals to you and seems doable, and then do it. Next, select another challenge. Many of these listed items may be done repeatedly, so do not do something just once and quit. Keep at it. The beginning of each school year is a new starting point, and the list begins all over again.

1. Have an article about the program published in the school paper.
2. Have an article about the program published in a local newspaper or magazine.
3. Have a local news station feature your program.
4. Have a local television program feature your program and include a performance.
5. Get invited to rehearse, conduct, and/or perform at a feeder school or neighboring district school.
6. Write an article about guitar education for a professional music education journal.
7. Perform in the community as a soloist or with other professionals.
8. Be accepted to speak at a state Music Education Association (MEA) conference.
9. Be accepted to speak or present at a national music education conference.
10. Be interviewed by a national music magazine or journal.
11. Be recognized by your school as an outstanding teacher or teacher of the year.
12. Be recognized as teacher of the year by your school district.

13. Be recognized as an outstanding music educator by professional education organizations.
14. Write and publish a book or other educational materials.
15. Be a guest on a podcast.
16. Present at conferences, conventions, and trade shows.
17. Run for office for the state MEA.
18. Run for office for the national MEA.
19. Actively seek opportunities for your ensembles to perform.
20. Actively seek festivals in which your ensembles may participate.
21. Build and maintain a website.
22. Be active on social media.
23. Attend professional development related to guitar/innovative education.
24. Network with other guitar/innovative teachers.
25. Mentor new teachers.
26. Create a YouTube channel.
27. Create good relationships with music equipment vendors and suppliers.
28. Seek composers to write original works for your ensembles.
29. Seek outstanding guitar educators to visit your school and work with your students.
30. Think big and outside the box. In this case, the box is the four walls of your classroom.

What Are Students Doing?

You can cultivate the reputation of your program around student performance, but as mentioned earlier, be aware that students are constantly changing. Seniors graduate; students move or change electives. Sports coaches, for instance, can easily recall the year or years of their best teams or championship teams. Music educators will also have years in which the ensembles are excellent and years in which that is not so much the case. It is the "not so much" years that we want to change. Ultimately, we want every ensemble to sound fabulous.

There will be years when all of the stars are in alignment and there will be a high level of performers and a high percentage of really serious students. The program will have outstanding soloists, remarkable small groups, and an incredible large ensemble. Naturally, you will want to apply for conferences, conventions, and trade shows during these years, using the recordings of these high-level groups. Yet many of these students will have moved on by the time these future events are scheduled. Your program may be accepted for next year's event and, meanwhile, your highly motivated upper classmen will be all or mostly all graduating!

This is the reason that building an award-winning program cannot rely solely on innate student talent. Jealous directors often point to those with award-winning programs and explain their rivals' success by claiming that all of the talented students attend that particular school. The reality is that the students *become* talented while attending a school with an award-winning program.

As with you, however, your students can take steps to gain recognition for your program. If there is an honor guitar ensemble in place, make sure to encourage students to participate. Each year make it public how many students auditioned and how many students were accepted. For example, if only two students audition and both are accepted, then your students have a 100 percent acceptance rate. That statistic is something to make public. It is also possible that you have twenty-five students accepted and the program accepted only forty students in total. Then, your students collectively make up 63 percent of the entire honor ensemble. Again, make it public and let your successes and those of your students be known and celebrated.

The same is true with solo and ensemble. Celebrate the numbers and make them known. Celebrate all successes. The more you can make your students feel special, the more special they will become. Success becomes perpetual if it is celebrated.

Defining a Line of Excellence

What happens when you get the opposite of a "stars align" type of year when students are collectively brilliant, the performance ensemble can take on particularly challenging music, and everything just runs smoothly? What if you instead find yourself in a situation one year in which your students are collectively unmotivated and will not practice? Maybe there are behavior issues, and everything becomes a challenge, as may happen to any educator. The question here is how a program can be good even during a low-performance year. The follow-up question is if it's possible to make a low-performance year appear to the public and to administrators as a high-performance year.

The answer to both is yes, but only if you establish a defined line of excellence that is never compromised.

On the basis of conversations I have had with struggling teachers, I have found it is usually obvious that their classes are missing many elements of guitar education. The one that is almost always absent is a defined line of excellence. But what does that entail?

Clearly defining the skills that every student must learn is a part of defining a line of excellence. For example, every student will learn to read music and to sight-read accurately. In addition, all students will learn scales in every key. The list goes on and on. What are the minimum skills required to have an award-winning guitar program? This is the question that every director must answer and maintain. Without a well-defined line of excellence, the possibility of having an excellent program any given year is strictly left to chance. Consider using the National Association for Music Education (NAfME) Council for Guitar Education's outline of guitar best practices for each year of study, as may be found on the NAfME website. (See Appendix B: NAfME Council of Guitar Education Guitar Best Practices.)

Thorough exposure to and familiarity with guitar repertoire and guitar ensemble literature is also a big plus when you are defining a line of excellence. What ensemble pieces sound great, but are not technically or rhythmically challenging? (See Appendix C: "Guitar Ensemble Repertoire" for music suggestions.) Every director should have a collection of ensemble pieces that sound really good, provided students perform the correct pitches and rhythms. Audience members will not know if your ensemble is performing a level-three, -four, or -five piece and will not care. They will hear only great-sounding music performed with a high level of musicianship: that is, if the director programs the music correctly and instills musical interpretations to the music. Some years it will be possible to play level-five or higher pieces. Other years may mean playing levels three and four. This reference to levels is based on level one as the easiest and level seven as the most difficult.

All performances must, regardless of levels, maintain a standard of excellence and musical expression, and directors should be familiar with strong performance pieces in each of the levels.

How do you find your defined line of excellence? More and more successful secondary guitar programs are sharing performance videos on YouTube. This is a great resource for you to learn from other successful programs. Those interested may spend many hours in watching all of the available videos featuring student guitar ensembles. Various levels of skill will be available from elementary schools to universities and some professional groups. There will also be ensembles from all over the world that are playing a wide variety of music.

YouTube Tags for Guitar Ensemble

The following are some common tags that may make it easier to find videos. In the search bar of YouTube, type these words and see what comes up.

1. Guitar orchestra
2. Guitar ensemble
3. Guitar ensembles
4. Guitar quartet
5. Guitar ensemble music
6. Guitar programs in schools

If you are teaching another type of ensemble, simply replace the word "guitar" with the name of the ensemble being taught. It is amazing what you can find.

Watching these videos is a great way to audition music and to find models that will help shape your own program. While watching these performances, consider where the line of excellence is defined for each group. Some will have a much higher line than others. Where do you want your line to be?

Here is a list of things to consider when you are watching ensembles and defining where the line of excellence should be.

1, Performance attire: Are the members of the ensemble in some type of uniform? Overall, do they look neat and stage appropriate?
2. Skill level: Is the selected piece being performed at a level of appropriateness for the skill level of the ensemble? Are students performing with complete control and accuracy? Are you hearing any obvious mistakes?
3. Difficulty of music: Is the music representative of the grade level of the student performers? Is it too hard, too easy, or just right?

4. Intonation: Is the ensemble in tune both in the upper and lower registers?

5. Music interpretation: Is the ensemble performing with period correctness, dynamics, and phrasing together with good overall musicianship?

6. Sitting position: Are all of the members of the ensemble sitting in classical position? If not, are all of the members sitting and holding the guitar the same?

7. Left-hand technique: Are all of the students playing on their fingertips? Do you see protruding left thumbs?

8. Right-hand technique: Are students playing with nails or picks? Is the ensemble producing adequate tonal quality? Are there strong contrasts in dynamics and timbre changes?

9. Overall preparation: Does the ensemble project a feeling of preparedness? Do ensemble members seem confident? Does the music sound well rehearsed?

10. Memorization: Is the music memorized?

These are considerations when you are evaluating an ensemble performance. It is important for you as the director to define where each of these areas needs to be to reach your line of excellence.

Networking

For a music educator who is building an award-winning program, learning the art of networking is an important piece of the puzzle. Networking is the process of interacting with others to exchange information and develop professional contacts. A major reason that professional groups host conventions is so that its members can get to know one another, exchange ideas, and be of assistance to one another in the future.

If you teach for a public school district, your district will most likely have its own email system in which you will be able to use a music educators' mailing list to contact all music teachers who are part of your district school system. Networking should start in your own geographic area. Become familiar with other educators teaching the same subjects as yourself. Visiting with like teachers is a great way to learn.

In addition to local teachers in your school district and neighboring districts, reach out to educators who are active or hold leadership positions in your state's MEA. Knowing your state leaders is helpful in the event you would like to see changes made, particularly if you want to advocate for more inclusive opportunities for your students in innovative ensembles.

You do not need to network only with teachers who teach the same age or level. If you teach high school, network with middle school teachers and community-college, college, and university teachers who teach in your field. This networking can be useful for the purposes of recruiting and feeding into other programs (discussed in greater detail in Chapter 5).

There are a number of professional organizations designed for networking. If you are not yet a member of these groups, consider joining. Attending state and national conferences for these organizations is a great way to meet new people in your field and increase your visibility. For music educators, the largest professional group to consider is NAfME. When you join NAfME, you will also be joining your state's MEA. Don't just join large organizations, however. Also consider more targeted organizations. Music educators who specialize in teaching string instruments, for instance, might join the American String Teachers Association, or ASTA. For those who specialize in teaching guitar, consider joining the Guitar Foundation of America, or GFA. For those music educators who specialize in commercial music, consider joining the National Association of Music Merchants, or NAMM. If you are teaching percussion ensemble, consider joining the Percussive Art Society, also known as PAS.

Attending the annual conferences of these organizations can be a lot of fun. These conferences are well organized and offer concerts, professional performances, classes, workshops, and opportunities to meet new people and greet folks you may already know and have not seen since the last conference. In addition, the conferences are ideal for growing your network, increasing your contacts, and becoming better known by others around the country.

Social media platforms like Facebook have professional groups related to music. For insight on how many groups exists, simply type in the word "guitar" in the search engine of Facebook and be amazed at the number and specificity of groups. There is a group specifically for school guitar teachers which may be found at: (https://www.facebook.com/search/top/?q=school%20guitar%20teachers). You can ask to join this group if you have a school email address and are actively teaching guitar in a secondary school. Once in, you may discover that other members face the same challenges you do. It is a place to post, ask questions, and receive professional responses.

This group, like most groups, offers an opportunity to network. While in Facebook, search any innovative ensemble. There are Facebook groups for percussion, jazz, rock band, mariachi, handbells, barbershop, and music technology, among others. You are very likely to find a supportive group on Facebook in which to network, regardless of which subjects you are teaching.

YouTube is a terrific resource for becoming familiar with innovative repertoire, other ensembles, and schools teaching innovative music at the secondary level. This platform is an excellent networking tool and a great place to learn about programs that are similar to yours. Take the time to reach out and send an email to the director, introduce yourself, and ask questions or simply compliment the program. To build an award-winning program, you have to let people know who you are. It is always best if they also think of you as being a nice person.

You can also follow other forms of media, such as newsletters, blogs, and podcasts. Make a point of learning about the many options available for you for communicating with others who share your interests, especially other music educators. Maybe you will be motivated to start one of your own forms of communication. There are so many ways to reach out and take advantage of the opportunities to make a concerted effort to let others know who you are and what innovative activities your students are doing, so that you don't go unnoticed. This effort is especially important if you have an award-winning program and live in a rural area . You can also invite guests to visit your program and hire professionals to come to your school. Keep networking toward the top of your perpetual to-do list.

The Benefits of a Strong Presence on YouTube

How many people normally see a single performance of one of your concerts? The answer used to be as many people as possible who can fit into the venue of the performance. That answer still holds true for the number of people who can see an event live and in person, but the number of people who can watch a recording later is endless. With YouTube, your performances may be seen around the world on any day at any time.

For creating an award-winning music program, it is important to have documentation of outstanding performances, world premieres, and debuts. For students who are thinking about attending your school and want to know what the music program is like, having visibility on YouTube makes it easy for prospective students to evaluate and prepare to audition for your program. The same is true about prospective faculty members who may be considering taking a job at your school.

Having a YouTube channel with documented videos of performances increases the perception that you have a strong, well-established program. Quality performances on YouTube are themselves accolades that may be seen far beyond the walls of your classroom and are capable of catching the attention of viewers from around the world. Just as importantly, your students and their parents can easily share links to videos with friends and family members. You can also share video links on websites, newsletters, blogs, and emails. YouTube makes it possible to share your successes with people who may not have the opportunity to visit your classroom.

Many global composers do not teach guitar but compose for guitar ensemble. With professional notation software like Finale and Sibelius, it is possible for composers to hear what their work sounds like by using the playback functions of these software programs. The sounds produced by this type of software, however, are electronic, and computer generated. Instead, some composers will record each part of a new ensemble in their studios and mix the channels together to hear their pieces played on real instruments, but this process is difficult and time consuming. Ultimately, composers want to hear their music performed by live musicians in real time in ensembles that perform together regularly.

Having a high profile on YouTube makes it easy for composers from around the world to find you. Many composers send their new music to directors with YouTube profiles in the hopes they will perform their music and post it online. Once on YouTube, videos can easily be shared in social media, emails, newsletters, and websites. One of the benefits of having a strong presence on YouTube is that you can be offered new music at no cost. What could be better than having noted composers send you music for free in exchange for performing it and putting it on YouTube?

A strong YouTube presence can attract attention from composers, but it can also garner emails from around the world with, for instance, questions about the music, the instruments, and the way the sound was created. It is always a surprise to hear from a guitar enthusiast from another country who is asking specific questions about how something was done in a performance video. Email contacts inspired by YouTube videos have spurred collaborations between schools, commissions with composers, college recruitments, invitations to perform, and a host of other opportunities.

Performance videos offer the opportunity to reach a national and international audience, and for you as a director to build a wider network of educators and enthusiasts.

Videos increase the discoverability of your program but also, importantly, make your performances accessible. Many students have family members who live in different cities or states, and some parents work at night and are not available to attend concerts. Having a video on YouTube is an easy way for students to share their performances with friends and family who otherwise would not have the chance to see them play.

Steps toward Creating a YouTube Channel

The single biggest task of creating a YouTube presence is having one or more cameras, a team of videographers, and the skills to film and edit. Luckily, more and more high schools are adding videography as an elective. If your school has such a program, this may be a resource for finding cameras as well as students to video-record your performances. If not, getting started may mean borrowing a camera and asking for a parent volunteer to video-record the performance.

Do not be discouraged if your school does not have a video program. Perhaps you can approach your school administrator with a proposal to introduce one. Many school administrators promote collaboration between programs. If the video program can work with the music department, then it can work with other departments in the school and be shared between departments in collaborative efforts. Hence it is a win/win for all involved.

Most students and adults own a cell phone and many of the newer smartphones have good-quality video cameras built in. The phone or camera should be placed on a tripod or other stabilizer in order to maintain a stable shoot. There are many such tripods and stabilizers available on the market.

Of the two philosophies about how to video-record a concert, one is to start the camera at the beginning of the performance and allow the camera to run continuously until the end of the concert. This is the easiest way to video. The challenge with this approach is the amount of time it will take to edit, because you will need to cut the breaks and pull out each individual performance. The end result should be one video for each selection of music rather than a continuous video of the entire performance. When viewers are searching on YouTube, typing a song title has a better chance of finding your video performance if each song has a separate video. If the song is included in a thirty-minute video, a search for the song title may not produce any results for your performance.

A number of studies have focused on viewing habits for videos. Collectively, these studies indicate that most consumers prefer videos that are six minutes or shorter. Studies further indicate that consumers may be reluctant to start a video that is more than five minutes long. Information found on each YouTube video indicates the number of minutes required to view the entire video. Posting an entire concert as one long video lessens its chance of being opened and viewed.

The second philosophy is to start and stop the camera at the beginning and end of each song performed. Though this method will take less time to edit, it takes much more effort and concentration on the part of the videographer. It also runs the risk of starting the camera late, stopping it too early, or not starting it at all.

Shooting the video of the performance is just the first step. Once the video has been recorded, it must be transferred from the camera or phone into a computer with some type of movie software capable of video editing. After the video has been downloaded into a movie editing software, the editing process begins. Editing is a skill within itself that can take as much or more time as filming the performance.

Apple computers come equipped with iMovie, which works well as a video editor. Windows has a free movie editor, Windows Movie Maker, which also does the trick. Other free movie-editing software programs include VideoPad Video editor, Filmora, Avidemux, and OpenShot. Though these free versions have limitations, they are capable of editing a live performance to be transferred to YouTube.

After the video is edited, it may be uploaded into YouTube. You will find a number of boxes to fill in as part of the process. The first box asks for the title, which will appear when viewers are searching for videos. It is common to put more information in this box than just the title: for example, the school name, the ensemble name, the song title, and the composer's name. The more information in this box, the easier it is for consumers to find during searching. And when viewers are watching this video, the information in this box is also visible.

The next box asks for a description, which can include the ensemble name, the school's name, the title of the performance piece, the composer, the arranger, the date, the conductor, the publisher, and any other pertinent

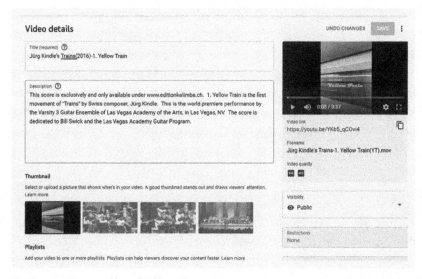

Figure 3.1 Screen shot of Yellow Train

information. When people watch the video, the information in this box is not visible, but it can be found underneath the video to give more information about what they are watching (for an example, see Figure 3.1).

If your video is a performance of a piece that is published and available for purchase, this box would be the place to mention who composed the piece and arranged the piece, and the details of the publication, including a link to the publisher's website. Including this metadata is a courtesy to the creative people who made the music available. It may help them sell more copies and it also makes it easier for other educators to find music they may like.

The next option is to provide a thumbnail similar to a book cover. YouTube will create one automatically, or you can also upload a JPG image that makes the video appear more professional. For example, this image may include the name of the ensemble, the name of the school, the title of the piece, and the composer. The title page is intended to sell or promote the content of your video. If this video is intended only for students and their parents, it may not be necessary to add a title page.

YouTube then asks if your video is made for young children. If your video is of a school performance, chances are your video is not made for kids younger than middle-school age. The next question is if you want to restrict your video to an adult audience. In most cases, the answer will be no.

The next box asks for tags. It will be these words that will help consumers find your video when they are searching. Your tags should include the school's name, the song title, the composer, the arranger, the publisher, and the conductor. Here are some additional tags used for school guitar ensemble videos: *guitar, guitar ensemble, guitar ensemble music, guitar trio, school guitar program, guitar music, guitar programs in schools, guitar ensembles,* and *guitar quartet*. These popular tags will help others find your video.

YouTube then gives the option of keeping your video *private, unlisted,* or *public*. Private maybe seen only by people who have been given the video code. Unlisted means that your video will not be found if someone is looking for it. Public means that it is listed and anyone on YouTube can find and watch it. There are reasons for all three. Pick the one that best suits your situation. In most cases, the choice will be *public*.

YouTube allows its users to create playlists. Assuming that you create one video per song, the playlist is a way to put all of the songs together in the order in which they were performed. This way, someone may watch the entire concert by selecting a playlist. When uploading videos, create a new playlist that is descriptive of the performance and includes the date as well. With each related video, select the playlist so the video may be added to it.

The following screenshot (Figure 3.2) is a YouTube playlist page. To the right of each playlist is a column entitled "Visibility" that indicates if the playlist is private, unlisted, or public. The next column shows the date the playlist was last updated. The final column indicates how many videos are in each of the playlists.

Figure 3.2 Screenshot of YouTube playlists

Once a video has been downloaded, YouTube will create a video link, which may be copied and pasted in, for instance, emails, social media, and websites. Anyone receiving this link may click it and watch the content of the video. This is a great way to promote your program. Also, YouTube will create a video link for the playlist once it is complete. Anyone with this link will be able to watch the entire content of the playlist.

YouTube offers ways to brand your program with banners, logos, websites, emails, and cards, even though they are not necessary just for listing a video for viewing. If you are thinking in terms of branding your program, how-ever, these promotional options are worth looking into and taking the time to do. It will make your program more visible to the world and will make your videos easier to find.

YouTube has numerous tutorials that demonstrate steps toward branding your program that go beyond the tasks of preparing and downloading a video for viewing. Here are a few titles to consider:

1. "How to Create a YouTube Channel"
2. "Starting YouTube: Do's and Don'ts for Beginners!"
3. "How to Add Tags to YouTube Videos"
4. "How to Create YouTube Channel Logo"
5. "How to Add a Featured Channel to Your Channel!"
6. "How Many Tags Are Allowed on YouTube"
7. "How to Make a YouTube Banner WITHOUT Photoshop!"
8. "How to Add YouTube Info Cards"
9. "How to Make a YouTube End Card Template"
10. "How to Create a FREE YouTube Logo 2020!"

Parent Consent

Before making videos of students and putting their images on the Internet, you must first get written consent from the parents. Students in a secondary public school will require a completed Publicity Consent Form signed by the parents even if a student is eighteen. Most schools have a preprinted form that gives parents the opportunity to allow their children to be photographed or video-recorded and their images used in public places such as magazines, posters, newspapers, banners, brochures, television, videos, and the Internet.

Without these completed forms, students should not be photographed or video-recorded. Early in the school year (generally the first week of school) is a good time to have this form completed and signed. A copy of this signed form should remain in your possession the entire school year, to protect you as the teacher and the school district that employs you.

A student who does not have consent must not be photographed. You may ask those students to step out of the picture. For videos, the faces of these students may be tiled, filtered, or blurred during the editing process. Check with your school administration regarding a Publicity Consent Form prior to any video-recording or photography.

Students under the age of thirteen are protected by the Federal Trade Commission under the Children's Online Privacy Protection Act. At the time of this writing, a school may be fined up to $43,280 per child for publishing photos or videos of students without a signed parental consent form. Do not invite a fine or a lawsuit. Insist on parents signing the forms, make copies, store them in a binder, and keep the binder in a safe, secure place. (See Appendix D, "Consent Form.")

4

Concerts and On-Campus Performances

Having sat through countless faculty meetings while I was listening to academic teachers express the challenges of teaching, I have always thought, "How about putting all of your students on a stage in front of all of their parents and friends and demonstrating your effectiveness as a teacher?" Though I have never verbally shared that idea, I have often thought how different it is to be a fine arts teacher who is expected to do these tasks. It has caused me to think long and hard about why performances are so important.

Learning to play a musical instrument lends itself by its nature to performing in front of others. That is just one part of the picture. Performing as an ensemble teaches its members collaboration, teamwork, self-confidence, and belonging to an organization that is larger than yourself. Donning the performance uniform transforms individuals into team players. Teamwork makes the dream work.

Performing, a core part of every music program, is an avenue to showcase students' skills and progress. Performing in front of an audience is an expectation for most music programs. In addition, performances are a bonding experience for all involved. Many details preparing for a performance are included in this chapter, including tips for developing a concert season and attracting community audiences to formal concerts, the steps to prepare for a performance, and ideas for additional on-campus performances.

Creating a Concert Season

Some schools set their performance calendars in the spring for the next school year. This way, events that occur in the summer or early in the school year, such as band camp or summer theater, are placed on the calendar ahead of time and the entire next school year is mapped out prior to the end of the current year. It takes some planning to do so and requires thinking ahead, but it is well worth the effort.

Building an Award-Winning Guitar Program. Bill Swick, Oxford University Press. © Oxford University Press 2022.
DOI: 10.1093/oso/9780197609804.003.0004

Many professional performing venues, for instance, will start advertising events months before they are scheduled to occur so that patrons can secure the date and plan ahead. School events should not be handled any differently. Families need to know about performance dates so that they do not purchase airline tickets or plan other events. Required performance dates should be set and communicated to students and their families months in advance, if at all possible, to avoid conflicts.

There are other ideas that we can learn from professional theaters and performance spaces. Professional venues often create a theme to their performance season and select shows that go along with that theme. Doing so makes the season more interesting and cohesive, and lets patrons know that there will be fresh shows that are connected to one another via the underlying theme. When developing a concert program for your school, why not also pick themes and offer a performance season instead of a number of random, unrelated shows? Why not promote the image that all of your performances during the year are in some way connected? Some music educators have been known to present the exact same programs year after year. Doing so means that your audience will not be as excited about attending. There is no pleasure in sitting through the same predictable holiday program for three or more years in a row, especially for families with multiple children in a music program. Similarly, playing the same music over and over again will draw less attention and interest from your administrators, faculty members, other students, and community members who may otherwise be interested in seeing your ensemble perform. Come up with something new for each performance, keep it fresh, and advertise that it is going to be different from previous performances.

Innovative problems do not mean, however, that you cannot recycle good ideas. For instance, you might establish annual productions, the way theaters will bring *The Nutcracker* to the stage every December. Your October performance could have an annual Halloween theme, or an Oktoberfest theme. December can always be a holiday show that features music of the season.

One school where I was teaching was having its tenth anniversary, and effort was being made to make the celebration last the entire year. The fine arts department decided to create a concert series titled *Ten Years of Excellence*. It was agreed that we would include highlights of previous performances into this series so that, throughout the year, audiences would be exposed to some of the best music performed during the first ten years of the school. The concept was such a success that we decided to continue with themed concert series.

The same school organized an international trip every three years. The first trip was to Spain. For two years, our concert seasons included Spanish music and music by Spanish composers. The next trip was to Austria, and for two years our concert seasons included music by Austrian composers. We would talk about the music and the opportunities for our students to travel to these destinations. The series created excitement and made fund-raising a little easier. Between the trips, the school celebrated its fifteenth anniversary, and we did another season of *Fifteen Years of Excellence*. One year, the school added a new musical theater program. To make our audiences aware of this addition, we did a concert season of popular titles from musicals.

The main idea is to create a performance season for the entire school year as early as possible—ideally, during the spring of the previous year. By then, your performance dates should be solid; the themes of the shows should be solid. Then it is just a matter of putting together promotional materials that display each of the programs in one pamphlet, poster, or flyer. This way, everyone knows when the performances will be for the entire year, and parents and students can start telling their friends and family about the upcoming events and encouraging people to come.

Community Audiences

Generally speaking, there are two main groups of audiences for your concerts. The largest group represents family members and friends of the students who are performing. Family often proves to be very supportive in attending performances while their children are involved with the program but tend to disappear once the children have left. Because the students at schools are constantly changing year to year, this audience will also change as students leave school programs and their family/friends also stop supporting school performances. For ease of understanding, we can refer to this audience as the temporary audience.

The smaller audience group can be thought of as a more permanent audience. School programs are often free or have minimal admission costs, and these events can be a good draw for community members looking to be entertained at a reasonable price. These members of the community attend performances because they like the programs and enjoy seeing children perform, even though they are not kin or in any way connected to the students.

Your temporary audience of friends and family is relatively easy to reach, but your community audience is more challenging to communicate with and needs more effort. To reach this audience requires using tools like community billboards, neighborhood newspapers and magazines, local radio and television broadcasts, and library poster boards. Capturing this audience also requires organization and a well-planned calendar with deadlines for submitting news releases and meeting publications dates. Often members of this audience will attend future performances and bring additional people with them. Over time, your program will become an important part of the community and not just a school-related program supported by parents of students.

Months before each concert, part of my preparation is to create a media release for the many magazines and newspapers in the community. Each publication has its own deadline and publication guidelines. Getting an early start makes it possible for us to meet the requirements for the various publications that provide a community calendar and include school events at no cost. In addition, our university radio station has a weekly events calendar and promotes school performances at no cost. We are fortunate enough to also have a local classical public radio station that promotes local classical music performances. There is a nominal fee for this service, but the station's audience is typically the audience we are also interested in capturing.

Building an audience from the community requires more effort than attracting the parent audience. However, community members tend to be long term, tend to tell others, encourage others to attend, and are likely to contribute financially if asked. In addition, community audience members frequently reach out to help or to volunteer.

Fifteen Steps toward a Performance

Here is a list of steps that may be involved in preparing for a performance. This will be a traditional, basic school ensemble concert. The steps required to do a basic concert often require assistance from the administration, faculty, and staff.

Step 1: Decide on a Theme for Your Performances

Earlier we discussed the benefits of building a thematic concert season. Yet whether your performance is a part of a concert season or not, it may still have a theme. A theme may be centered on a time period or style. One example of a theme might be *Music from around the World*, and each piece performed would be written by a composer from a different country. Another example could be *Playing the Classics*, featuring music from the Classical period and possibly the Romantic period. Other ideas may include *An Evening of Show Tunes*, *The Music of Cole Porter*, *An Evening with Rogers and Hammerstein*, *Bach to Beatles*, or *Music by Eric Clapton*. Before deciding on a theme, make certain that you have or can acquire the necessary amount of music to do an entire concert tied to the selected theme.

A concert theme for guitar might be *A Classic Rock Concert*, which would feature popular music from the 1960s, 1970s, and 1980s. Or perhaps the theme is an annual one like *A Holiday Concert*, featuring music tradition-ally associated with the month of December. Perhaps you would like to do *An Evening with the Beatles*. Other ideas for themes might include *400 Years of Guitar Music*, *Television Theme Songs*, *Movie Soundtracks*, *Video Game Music*, *Music by Johnny Mercer*, *Picking on Bach*, *Swinging Jazz*, and *Country Hits*. Take inspiration from these ideas to develop your own theme in order to create a purposeful performance.

Step 2: Select Your Music

Once you have selected the theme, begin picking arrangements that will fit the theme. There is an art to selecting music, but before you even begin to think about which songs will fit your theme, you need to know the length of the performance and thus how much music will be needed to fill the allotted time.

For instance, consider that an average song is three minutes. If you will be performing for an hour, you will need about sixteen songs to fill the time. With two ensembles planning to perform the same amount of time, each will need about eight selections to collectively fill a one-hour performance. If there are three ensembles, the first ensemble—assuming it is of the youngest students—may perform for fifteen minutes and need only four songs. The second ensemble may perform twenty minutes (about six songs) and the third ensemble may perform twenty-five minutes (about seven songs). Doing this math gives you an idea of how much material will be needed to fill the time (seventeen songs).

When selecting music, always pick more music than needed for a couple of reasons. I generally select two additional pieces per ensemble. Students will respond in a variety of ways to the selected music. If there is something your students really like, they will work hard on it and make an effort to really learn it. The reverse is also true: students are not apt to put as much effort into pieces they do not like. Keep in mind that students will not be equally excited about every piece. If you select more music then needed, then you can program only the music the students respond well to. It is important to remain flexible and adapt to your students' interests. After a couple of weeks of rehearsals, you may need to replace pieces that students are unenthusiastic about. It is also possible that you selected music in the first round that is too hard or too easy. Be mindful that your first round of music selection may need adjustments, and that is okay.

The organization of your library will determine how you will select your music. I have my entire library in PDF files. From a computer, I can see what titles are available and send the files straight to the school's graphic artist, who will print them and make copies for me.

Our band, choir, and orchestra teachers store each arrangement in a manila folder and place them in filing cabinets in alphabetical order. They also maintain a printed list of titles that makes it easy to see what music is available. When the teachers request titles, the office assistant pulls the folders and makes any copies that are needed.

If you are in need of music, www.sheetmusicplus.com is a good resource for popular music. The sites of www.JWPepper.com and www. Guitarintheclassroom.com are good resources for music from the five major historical periods, for traditional dances and folk music, and for traditional guitar repertoire.

Step 3: Print Your Music

Once you have selected the music it will need to be copied for distribution. Before making copies of any music, make certain that no copyright laws are being broken. Some publishers sell music in a PDF format and offer a purchasing agreement to make as many copies as needed for performance purposes. Other publishers will require customers to purchase as many copies as necessary, so students are playing from a hard copy from the publisher. Do not assume that free music found on the Internet may be copied or publicly performed. Be responsible when it comes to following copyright laws.

Provided you are following copyright laws, this will be an opportunity to visit the graphic artist/printer at your school and request copies. The graphic artist/printer will have a procedure for ordering copies that will be important to become familiar with and accurately follow.

Before you can request copies, however, it is important to know how many students are in each of your ensembles and how many parts each arrangement is written for. If there are thirty-two students in an ensemble, for instance, and the arrangement is written in four parts, then you will need eight copies of each part. If the arrangement is written in three parts, there will be a need for eleven copies of each part.

When ordering copies, request that the parts are three-hole punched. This way, students can drop their music into a three-hole binder. The music should remain in their binders and the binders should be at every rehearsal and performance. The three-hole binder should be a required accessory for the class.

Step 4: Distribute Your Music

There are a number of ways to distribute music to students. Here are two ideas to consider before choosing the best way to distribute music.

1. Random mixture: Though this is not a popular choice for most directors, a random mixture means that students sharing the same parts do not sit together, but parts are randomly distributed throughout the ensemble. This type of distribution has many pluses. No matter where a student is sitting, each student, as they play, will likely be able to hear the other parts, too. The ensemble will sound more blended because the parts are spread throughout the ensemble. Finally, this method requires students to count and read more independently.

Distribution for a random mixture can be done as a reward. For example, the first student to come to class on the day of distribution gets first pick. The last person gets what is left. Distribution may be done by grades. The students with the highest grades get first pick and students with the lowest grades get what is left. There are many other ways to allow students to choose parts. For example, seniors may be the first to pick, first chair students may get first selection, you may decide to go through different ends of the alphabet allowing students with the last name starting with the letter "A" or "Z" go first, and there are other creative ways to randomly distribute music.

2. Sections: Distributing music by sections is the most popular with directors. With this approach, students sharing the same part all sit close to one another. If the director wants to hear all of part ones, simply point to that section and rehearse just the students playing part one. Each student with part one hears other students playing the same part, an approach that may help with note reading and rhythms.

When passing out multiple arrangements, make the decision if the same students are going to receive part one for each of the songs or if each section gets various parts to all of the music. For example, if you are distributing four titles, each section will have one part one, one part two, one part three and one part four. Every student then has the opportunity to perform a part one. Or you may create a system wherein a select group of students receive all of the part ones and another group will get all part twos, and so on.

Step 5: Preparing Your Ensemble through Rehearsals

Every director will have an individualized method for rehearsing their ensemble. Most ensemble preparation will be done during the scheduled music classes during the school day. Directors should have an idea how many weeks it will take to prepare an ensemble for a performance. At this stage it should be apparent how many songs will be needed to be prepared. If it will take more than seven weeks to get students ready for a performance, this is an indicator that the music selected is too difficult. If students are ready to perform after two or three weeks, the selected music is probably not quite difficult or challenging enough. If after two weeks the ensemble is sounding performance ready, you will need to bring in different music that is more challenging. On the other hand, if after four weeks the ensemble still cannot perform a piece well, you will need to replace it with something less challenging. Do not hesitate to make these changes, depending on the prog-ress of your ensembles.

Step 6: Promote the Performance Date and Program

Chances are that the date for your performance was selected before the school year began. If that is not the case, it will be important to make sure all of your students, as well as their parents, are aware of the date. Otherwise, it is certain there will be conflicts. Visit the administrator who is in charge of ac-tivities and request that the date be included on the school website, as well as the parent communication forum, which may be a regular email and/or re-corded phone message. If you maintain a website for your program, promote the performance dates on this site as well.

Step 7: Communicate through a Group Organizer App

It will be helpful to use a group organizer app such as Sign-Up Genius, a free online software tool for volunteer management and event planning. There are other apps such as Volunteer.com, 353 Online Roster System, Signup.com, Signupzone.com, Timecounts, Track it Forward, and Volunteerlocal. Find one that you like. It will be important to input the email addresses of the parents of your students. This effort takes time but needs to be done only once a school year. Once you have loaded the emails, you can begin commu-nicating with your parents. Doing so is a way to announce the performance date of the concert and an opportunity to list everything for which help is needed and give parents an opportunity to sign up for specific tasks. These tasks may be any of the steps listed moving toward preparation for a concert.

Step 8: Meet with the Theater Manager

Some schools have full-time theater managers. Other schools assign administrators or faculty the duty of manager of the theater. Some schools require music directors to complete a form that will indicate the needs of the ensemble for a performance. Meet early with the individual in charge of the theater facility to discuss your requirements, such as the number of chairs and stands, the sound system, and the lighting. Also indicate if there will be tickets sold, how and where they will be sold, and who will be selling them, and if there will be chaperones, ticket takers, program distributors, and/or ushers.

Discuss the stage setup and provide a seating chart to illustrate the placement of each of the chairs and music stands. Have an idea of how many microphones will be needed and what type of lighting you would prefer. Also discuss the details of what should occur immediately following the performance. Does the stage need to be cleared? Do chairs and stands need to be stacked and returned to designated area? Do these tasks need to occur immediately after the performance, or can some of them be done the following day? Be as detailed as possible in your planning and have an idea how much help you will need to set up and break down your performance.

Discuss in detail with the theater manager what type and how many microphones are available through the theater. The acoustics of the theater will play a big part in how much sound reinforcement will be needed. Some theaters have hanging microphones centered above the performing ensemble. In many cases, that arrangement will be all that is needed. For guitar ensembles, condenser microphones work well if more sound reinforcement is needed. A large guitar ensemble may need four to eight additional microphones, depending on the acoustics and the size of the performing space.

Step 9: Create a Poster

Weeks before the scheduled concert, consider creating a promotional poster. Most school printers can print an 11" × 17" poster. This size is more than adequate and may be printed either landscape or portrait. The poster should have an image that captures the theme of the performance. The text should include the title of the concert with all of the specifics, including the location, the actual address, the date and time, the performers, and the price of admission if there is one. If not, your poster should indicate that admission is free.

Posters may be printed weeks before the event and distributed by students to such venues as libraries, music stores, classrooms, businesses, restaurants, and bookstores. These posters will be an important tool to build your community audience. Moms and Dads will likely come whether there is a poster or not, but people in the community will attend only if they are aware a concert is happening.

Directors may send posters through school mail to other schools. In part of a networking effort, make sure the schools that feed your school receive an invitation to attend your concerts. Provide comps (free admission) to students and directors who attend from other schools. Encourage directors to consider giving extra credit or some incentive to encourage their students to attend your concerts. In return, you will do the same for their concerts.

Sending a concert poster to another school can be done electronically, which is the easiest, or you can send a physical poster through school mail. (See Chapter 10 for more information about how to publicize events electronically.)

Once again, you will need to visit your school graphic artist/printer to ask for assistance with this publicity. The poster should be created in a software program like Microsoft Publisher and saved as a PDF or a JPG file. Ask your graphic artist about the preferences for receiving the files.

The printer will be able to create colored posters from your files. I generally request about one hundred posters for the first run. Once the posters are complete, take about half of them to the office of the administrator who is in charge of activities. Though that office may have a student assistant who will hang posters around campus in all of the appropriate places, do not assume as much. The office in charge of activities is a good place to start. If this office cannot assist you, the staff will direct you to the office that may. Each school has its particular way of handling publicity for school activities.

Take the remaining posters to your classroom and instruct your students to ask permission to hang posters in their workplaces, local music stores, favorite restaurants . . . wherever the posters are likely to be seen. Also encourage students to hang posters inside their academic classrooms if their teachers will allow them to do so. If all the posters are taken, ask the printer for more.

Step 10: Create a Concert Program

Assuming your ensembles have had several weeks to rehearse and prepare for the upcoming concert, your students should be quite familiar with the music you have provided. It is important to allow your students to select their favorite pieces from the prospective repertoire you have given them, to allow them ownership of their performance. As an ensemble, choose the opening song and then the ending song for a strong opening and closing to the performance. Once those two have been selected, start with the pieces in the middle. Be mindful of tempos and styles of the pieces and turn the process into a lesson involving the entire ensemble.

The program should have the song titles, composers' names, and arrangers' names (if applicable), organized in the order in which the songs will be performed. In addition, the program should have the name of the venue, the date, and the title of the concert. The title of the concert could simply be "Guitar Concert," or it could reflect the theme that has been selected. For example, the title on the program could be "Picking on the Beatles."

Also included should be the names of each student performing. It is most important that each student's name is spelled correctly, listed completely, checked, double checked, and triple checked. Each teacher should have a class roster from the grade book, a good resource to check to make sure every name is included, is complete, and is spelled correctly. Nothing is worse than putting on a fabulous concert only to be met with an angry parent afterwards because a student's name is listed incorrectly or not at all. You can't do much to make up for this type of error except to make certain that it does not happen again.

Once the list of students has been typed and put into place on the program, print that page of the program and pass it around your classes. Insist that students see their names and make any corrections on the sheet that need to be made. Make the corrections, print the page, and pass it out again to make sure every student sees their name. Doing so will eliminate the possibility of many mistakes. In the event you have made a mistake on the program, it is easier to say to a parent that you passed it around on three different occasions to request changes. This precaution puts some of the responsibility on the student and makes it a little easier to deal with the parent.

The program should also include a listing of the school's administrators and music faculty. Your program may also include dates and details of upcoming events. There should be information how to join social media, YouTube channel information, website information, and the director's email and school phone number. Take this opportunity to explain how to join the parent booster club as well. Look at the program as a way to communicate with all of your parents.

The more professional a production appears, the more likely people will attend future performances. Whenever possible, consider printing a professional-looking program for the performances. Some schools even sell advertisements in the programs to cover the costs of printing programs.

Some schools have strict rules that require an administrator to proofread any and all written materials before they are printed. If those rules apply at your school, then provide a copy to the appropriate administrator with plenty of time for proofing.

Once everything has been checked and double checked in your program, it is now time to have the program printed. Here is another time you will need to visit the graphic artist/printer, who may have some ideas about how to make the program look more professional. Discuss with the printer how many copies of the program you will need. A rule of thumb is to multiply the number of students performing by the number four. It may not be exact, but it will be a starting point. If there are sixty-four student names on the program, there will be a need for 256 programs. At the end of the concert, you will be able to talk to your helpers and find out if there were programs left over or if there were not enough, so that you can adjust for the next performance. After going through this exercise a few times, you will learn what number to use to multiply the number of students performing. The number is likely to fall between three and five for performances requiring a paid admission. For free concerts, the number may be between four and eight.

The graphic artist/printer will need some time to prepare the program. Have a conversation ahead of time and see how much lead time is necessary so that you can pick up the completed program a day or two before your performance. It may be a week ahead of time. It may be ten days or two weeks. Check beforehand: do not take your job to the printer two days before your event and expect it to be completed on time. (See Appendix E: "Sample Program" for an actual program.)

Step 11: Sell Tickets

Though some schools do not allow an admission to be charged for school functions, other schools do. For some schools, it is the income from concert ticket sales that pays for such costs as programs, posters, strings, picks, music, and instruments. The list of expenses can go on and on.

Some schools use an electronic ticketing service for performances. This too makes your program look professional. Patrons can go to the ticketing site, pick their seats, purchase their tickets, and either print tickets or have them sent electronically to their phone. This process saves time at the box office the night of the performance and also provides an idea of how many tickets have been purchased prior to the performance, just to ensure there will be enough programs.

Though using such a service has many advantages, one of the best features is that the service collects information on everyone who purchases a ticket not only for your show, but also for every program provided at your school. This data collection adds to the possibility of growing the community audience. It is possible to send an email to everyone who has purchased a ticket in the past and inform them that there is an upcoming guitar concert. Some of these people may have never been to a guitar concert and may like to attend one out of curiosity. If they like it, they are apt to come to future ones. These patrons fall into the category of the community audience, the more permanent audience.

Step 12: Assign Ushers, Ticket Sellers, Program Distributors, Seaters

It is common for grandparents and/or cousins to attend school performances. Often this is the very first time they have been in the performing venue or even on the school campus. It can be confusing. Having ushers and/or chaperones stationed by the entrance, in the lobby, and in the seating area can look professional and be very helpful for assisting those who are visiting for the very first time.

If there will be more than one ensemble performing, have those students playing in the later ensemble up front covering the doors, lobby, and seating area until it is time to start the show. Have parent volunteers chaperone these students in the event an issue arises that needs the assistance of an adult.

If tickets are going to be sold the night of the performance, there will need to be a "bank," which means a starting amount of cash to be used as change. In most cases, the bank should start with one hundred $1 bills and twenty

$5 bills, for a total of $200. To have a bank requires meeting with the school banker and requesting a bank with specific denominations of bills. It will be necessary to collect the bank from the banker on the day of the performance. Any time money is involved, it will be necessary to have adults around, a task that can fall to the parent booster club. Ticket sellers should be arranged prior to the night of the performance. After all of the tickets have been sold, the administrator on duty for the evening will need to count the money and complete the paperwork associated with banking procedures for school events.

Step 13: Set Up a Reception

One of the advantages of hosting a reception, if there is going to be one following a performance, is that it gives parents an opportunity to see and talk to the director and to one another. It has the potential for a very social opportunity. You can even refer to it as "fellowship." It can include refreshments or not. Using the parent booster club is a good way to offer refreshments at a reception.

Step 14: Set Up a Videographer

If you want to have the performance video-recorded, it will be important to set up a videographer. If your school has a video class, contact the faculty member who teaches that class. Perhaps the teacher or some students will agree to video-record the performance. Otherwise, the parent booster club may offer a parent with the skills to video-record.

Step 15: Assign an Administrator and Custodian Team

The administrator in charge of activities will be the person to assign an administrator and custodian team to your concert. Though this task is not your responsibility, it will be important to contact the administrator and find out who will be working your concert. In the event you have a problem that requires action, these are the people to contact. If possible, have the contact information for the administrator and head custodian who will be on duty during your performance.

Perform, Perform, Perform

The previous sections have detailed the importance of and steps toward a formal performance. These formal on-campus concerts tend to draw a large audience and, if ticketed, can help to sustain the program financially. Yet informal concerts and performance opportunities on your campus also have their place in an award-winning program. Informal performances can elevate the profile of your program and inspire your peers to see you as a "player," one who answers the call from others when there is a need. In addition, those performances help with recruiting students and positioning your program in good (and more visible) standing with the administration.

From time to time, for instance, school administrators are confronted with opportunities to host special guests for breakfast or lunch. In these instances, they may be expected to make a room such as the library, gym, lecture hall, or cafeteria look attractive and hospitable by decorating, adding flowers, and of course, offering food. Sometimes an administrator will put in a request for a small music ensemble to perform for one of these functions. There is really only one answer if you are ever asked to do something like this: yes! It does not matter when it is, how soon it is, what is expected from the performance, the answer should always be an excited "yes"—that's why the exclamation mark!

Though this response seems simple enough, it has been a hard lesson to learn for many music educators. There can be a hundred reasons to say "no." You may have a planned playing test that day; there may not be enough time to rehearse an ensemble; it may be during your prep when you do not have students assigned to you. The excuses can go on and on, but there is no excuse not to say yes. Saying "yes" is always the best for your program. It does not matter how inconvenient it is or how hard you will have to work to make it happen. The opportunity for payback will happen soon enough. If the school receives extra funding in the future, it will be the programs that are supportive of the administration that receive any extra gifts or unexpected financial support. On the other hand, if you are always saying "no," when it comes time for you to ask something of the administration, you may be met with the same answer.

It is a simple lesson: when asked by an administrator to provide entertainment for any special event, always answer with an enthusiastic "yes!"

Ideas for Other On-Campus Performances

Most music educators agree that the more opportunities students have to perform, the better. Don't just wait to be asked by your administration to perform at school events—seek these events out. Your school may have annual events such as an annual tea for the faculty, an annual Renaissance festival, an annual chili cook-off... the possibilities are endless. Check with the administrator who is in charge of student activities for a complete listing of on-campus activities. As you look at this list, consider any of these events as possibilities for student performances. For example, students could perform at Open House, College-Fair Night, and Fall Carnival. Once your ensembles have been seen performing at these types of events, chances are good that faculty members will come up with other ideas for performances for your students. Parents and other visitors to campus may also have opportunities for your ensembles to perform.

You could also promote in-class performances. Ruth LeMay, an outstanding music educator from Minneapolis, Minnesota, agrees that students should perform as frequently as possible in as many settings as possible. She promotes playing in various ways such as formal, competitive, relaxed, peer, open mic, with/without conductor direction, and student-choice selections. LeMay schedules a day each week in class for open mic and encourages students to sign up for one of the spots available and perform the music they are working on at the time.

Another opportunity for in-class performances is to coordinate with the English department, which might have a prescribed reading list for each level of English classes. Make a point to get to know the teachers in the English department and discuss how music ensemble performances can be integrated in their literature lesson plans. Students may come to you and ask for music from a specific time period to match the historical period of the literature being read. See this request as a teaching opportunity and assist students with period music appropriate to what is needed in literature class. It will be an educational experience for all involved and another opportunity for students to perform in a classroom outside of the music room.

Some schools require faculty members to supervise students during lunchtime, known in the educational circle as lunch duty. Teachers tend to despise the days they are scheduled for this duty, even to the point of regularly taking those days off. Senior teachers with an accumulation of sick days can easily do so if they choose.

If you are faced with the unpopular task of doing lunch duty, consider asking some of your students to join you and perform during lunch. Students will love seeing their peers performing. The administration enjoys seeing students performing. The music can be entertaining and calming and bring joy to those who hear the performance. This proposal also makes doing lunch duty a good deal more tolerable, even enjoyable.

5

Using Feeder Programs, Recruiting Students, and Building Longevity

Students are always changing. Especially for secondary school teachers—who constantly receive students from elementary or middle school while also "feeding" students to high schools or universities—it is important to understand how students move from one school to another. How do you make the most of students who may be coming into your program, and how do you help students get into programs when they graduate from yours?

From time to time, teachers find themselves in a situation in which they are their own feeders. For example, for four years I taught half time at a middle school that fed into a high school where I taught the other half of the day. The high school students fed into the university, where I also taught. During that time, I had middle school students who became my high school students, and high school students whom I then taught at the university. I've since found others who have had similar experiences, and they all agree that feeding oneself is the ideal situation. Because students already know the teacher, they are more likely to continue with music. In many cases, continuity can also make the transition from one school to another easier.

Not every teacher, however, has the luck of feeding their own programs to maintain strong or at least steady enrollment numbers. Yet enrollment is key for any successful music program, and teachers should take active steps to make sure they are recruiting new students as well as maintaining current student engagement as much as possible. This chapter will emphasize the importance of recruitment, tips for recruiting and feeding into universities, and advice for how to build a self-perpetuating program.

Elementary to Middle School

Middle school band, orchestra, and choir directors depend heavily on the elementary schools that feed their middle school. It is not unusual for these

Building an Award-Winning Guitar Program. Bill Swick, Oxford University Press. © Oxford University Press 2022.
DOI: 10.1093/oso/9780197609804.003.0005

teachers to meet elementary music teachers and schedule visits to their schools in order to demonstrate instruments and encourage students to sign up for a music class as their elective choice. Middle school music teachers also rely heavily on the feeder elementary music teachers to teach students basics, such how to read music, how to count rhythms, and how to learn the fingerings or positions of an instrument. These skills are all preparation for moving into the middle school band or orchestra.

Some elementary teachers offer ukulele or guitar in the later years of elementary school, and thus help prepare students who would like to go into a middle school guitar class. Frequently, the middle school guitar teachers are also the band, choir, and/or orchestra teachers. These teachers may primarily promote band, choir, and orchestra, but if students are interested in guitar, the teachers will be able to answer questions. A middle school music teacher's main goal is to encourage as many students as possible to use their elective choice to join a music class.

For the most part, the message I've heard from middle school guitar teachers is that they have not needed to do much recruiting at elementary music schools. If you are one of those lucky teachers who fill your classroom without recruiting, good for you! Though the guitar may be quite popular in your area and at your middle school, however, recruiting can still be important. Your future students will benefit from having guitar class explained to them before they begin your program. Visits from elementary school students can also be opportunities to showcase that you are an accomplished teacher and that the content of your classes will be interesting.

When recruiting at an elementary school, take along a couple of guitars. As the teacher, be prepared to play for the students as you demonstrate how the guitar sounds and explain what skills you teach in your classroom. In the event that there are students who can already play guitar, have them perform on one of the guitars you bring and play along if possible, or you can provide some constructive hints about how to improve. Be sure to be positive and always offer encouragement to students to join your class. If possible, take along a couple of sixth-grade guitar students who recently graduated from the school you are visiting and have them play for these students. Allow them to answer as many student questions as possible.

This active recruitment may not be possible in your district. Many middle schools rely solely on the school counselors to do the recruiting. Often the elementary schools set a date in which the middle school counselors can come to distribute flyers and show a video featuring the possible electives, and that is the extent of middle school recruiting. If this sounds like your situation, you can still take steps so that your program is getting the most out of your school's recruitment activities. Make sure that your program is well represented in the recruiting video being used and is visible in all brochures or recruiting materials. This could be one of the many times that having a dedicated website and a YouTube channel may be beneficial. Visit with your recruiting counselor, provide links to your program's website, and share YouTube links of your best recorded performances. If possible, have this information printed in the recruitment brochures.

Middle School to High School

Recruiting middle school students for high school music programs is very important. Students often have only a handful of choices for electives while they are in middle school or junior high, and some students might have signed up for music classes only because there were not many other options. When middle school students move to high school, however, the number of elective choices seem endless. There may be electives such as robotics, animation, photography, music technology, video production, ceramics, ballroom dancing, and a host of other exciting choices that will compete for the students' interest and time, depending on the high school.

The following is an actual list of elective choices at the high school where I teach. Freshman have only one choice for an elective and must pick one class from this list: Advanced Jazz Combo, Advanced Small Guitar Ensemble, Beginning Guitar, Beginning Orchestra, Beginning Mariachi, Beginning Piano, Chorus I, Elective Concert Band, Elective Jazz Band, Handbells, History of Rock 'n' Roll, Men's Chorus, Modern Music Tech I, Modern Music Tech II, Music Theory, AP Music Theory, Musical Theater, Opera Workshop, Vocal Jazz, Philharmonic Winds, Symphony, Vocal Ensemble, Imaginative Writing, Journalism Foundations, Play Writing I, Play Writing II, Publications 1, Publications II, Ballet, Introduction to Modern Dance, Ceramics, Design Crafts, Film Studies, Graphic Design, Photography, Robotics, Studio Art, 3D Sculpture, Spanish I, Spanish II, Spanish III, Japanese I, Japanese II, Japanese III, and Chinese I.

The point of this list is to illustrate just how many options there are for freshman students at my high school, and they can pick only one! It is not unusual for an incoming freshman who has just completed three years of guitar in middle school to say, "I already know how to play guitar. I would like to do something different." And at that point, you may have lost the opportunity for this student to ever join your program. As a freshman who has just completed three years of middle school guitar class, this student likely has the skills to join an intermediate or advanced class in high school. If they skip guitar class in the ninth grade, however, this student may not practice guitar daily and will eventually lose skills. The result is that they may not place in an intermediate or advanced class when they consider taking guitar as a junior or senior, an outcome that may discourage them from joining the program. Students don't usually like to repeat beginning guitar class. Older students also don't usually like attending classes that are primarily filled with students from younger grade levels. If a student does not continue or begin guitar classes freshman year, the likelihood of taking guitar during the upper grades is slim.

If you are a high school teacher, recruiting incoming freshman needs to begin as early in the school year as possible. Each year, consider hosting a middle school honor guitar ensemble in which middle school students have an opportunity to come to your campus, play in an ensemble that you direct, and get a feel for the campus and your teaching style. Another idea may be to host a solo and ensemble festival for these students for which you are the judge. Host a middle school ensemble festival at which all of the middle schools in the district come to your campus and perform for one another. Or pick a Saturday and host a "Guitar Day" so middle school students can visit your school, spend time with some of the high school guitar students, play for one another, take private lessons, and end with a joint performance. Think of ways to get these students physically onto your campus and have some exposure to your style of teaching.

Another idea that has worked well in my experience is to set up a day and time that high school guitar students can visit the middle schools and possibly perform. Exposing middle school students to more advanced high school students can be aspirational. Each time there is a scheduled guitar performance at the high school, make sure to notify the middle school music teachers and send invitations and tickets to the students and their parents to encourage them to attend. Some high schools have a program referred to as "shadow day"—an opportunity for a middle school student to be paired with a high school freshman and attend a full day of school at the high school.

Check with your school counselors to see if there is an event like this one in place or if one can be planned.

Middle school students are already technically savvy and frequently pay attention to social media to make decisions about course selections and opportunities. It is important for a high school music teacher to have a high social media profile that remains within the parameters defined by your school district. If possible, have a dedicated guitar program website that includes upcoming concerts, recordings or videos of past performances, photos of students performing and having fun, documentation of trips, and a class handbook outlining class expectations and a list of skills that students will learn while in the program.

If possible, have a Facebook and/or Instagram page that is dedicated to just the guitar program. (Make sure to adhere to all school-related policies regarding social media.) Post achievements of your program and give incoming students reasons for wanting to be a part of it.

In Chapter 3, we discussed creating a YouTube channel featuring videos of your students performing. This is another way to reach students via social media. In addition to performance videos, you might also post videos of your teaching skills. Give prospective students reasons to want to be in your class. Show them that your program is something special.

High School to College

Most schools will assume that almost all high school students want to continue their education and go to college—or at least, they will promote the idea that students *should* continue their education. High school counselors often start talking to students about college selection as early as their sophomore year. By junior year, high school students should be making serious efforts to select schools and gather what they need to apply for their desired schools.

The study of guitar in college is relatively new. Some colleges are just now adding degree opportunities in guitar, and many universities still do not offer guitar as a major. US colleges first began offering degrees in guitar in the 1960s, but it wasn't until the 1980s that the momentum picked up, and many more universities added guitar to their catalogs. Because the inclusion of guitar at universities was so new in the 1980s and 1990s, there were ample students with the desire to seriously study guitar. For many universities, recruiting for guitar students simply was not necessary.

As guitar studies have become increasingly popular in public schools, there are now more high school seniors with advanced guitar skills than ever before. Continuing their studies and majoring in guitar in college no longer has the sparkle it once did. We are living in a time when there are no longer any obvious guitar heroes or visible celebrity guitarists on television or in the movies. The popular music landscape has changed as well, and the business of recording, producing, and selling music has become much more complicated. High school seniors and their parents are not seeing obvious career paths as a guitarist, and university guitar programs are no longer attracting the numbers they once did. It is now time to learn to recruit.

Because I teach at a performing arts school, I have been blessed with having talented students who are attractive to university guitar programs. For that reason, I have witnessed a variety of approaches to recruitment. The most popular attempt is for a university to send their top guitar teacher to our campus to meet students and perform for them. Though hosting some of the top teachers in the country on our campus has been great, the once-a-year performance is not the most productive approach to recruiting.

The most effective recruiter I have worked with is Matt Denman, currently at Oklahoma City University. He makes a point of visiting our campus two or three times every year. He schedules his visits during our quarter concerts to hear student performances, meets the students, learns their names, and has an opportunity to comment on their performance the next day when he meets with them. In addition, Denman schedules visits to take parents of interested students to breakfast and/or lunch to get to know them and also give them an opportunity to get to know him. In addition, Denman hosts an annual guitar festival that includes activities and competitions for high school and college students held on his campus in Oklahoma. Each year, we receive an invitation to attend, and it gives our students an opportunity to visit his school. Denman's approach to recruiting has been most successful. He holds the record for recruiting the most students from our program.

All of the same elements used by high school directors to recruit middle school students apply to university programs. There should be a dedicated website with current information about the program, a YouTube channel with student and faculty performances, a Facebook page posting photos of students having fun, an Instagram page, and an annual festival involving high school students.

When I first started writing this book, the world was in lockdown because of the COVID-19 pandemic. Most schools in the United States were closed, and students and teachers were dependent on technology for distance learning. Almost all students in the United States are now very familiar with platforms like Zoom, Canvas, and Google Meets. This turn of events has evolved into a perfect climate in which schools can recruit virtually. There are no travel expenses involved in virtual recruiting, so college faculty members have the opportunity to regularly connect with potential students anywhere in the United States.

Colleges also rely heavily on college fairs for recruiting. Colleges have full-time recruiters who attend college fairs and are able to answer questions about their schools. As a reference, https://www.musicadmissionsroundta ble.org/ is a good resource for many of the universities that offer music degrees. Once on the site, select "College Fairs." In 2021, all college fairs were held virtually. Time will tell if college fairs return to how they were previously, or if the elements adopted during the pandemic continue to be used in the future. Colleges are likely to combine the best of both approaches.

Self-Perpetuating Programs

Here is a simple question that often receives odd responses. If you were asked how many students leave your program each year, what would your answer be? Another way to ask the same question would be how many new students you need to attract each year to replenish the number of students leaving. Though the question seems straightforward, few teachers seem prepared to answer it.

Teachers often complain about large class sizes and the distribution of students. The biggest complaint is that the advanced class has intermediate-level students in it. An even bigger complaint is that every class has mixed levels of skill. The problem is most often the result of teachers not having a handle on how many students are leaving the program at each level and how many students are needed to keep classes balanced both in numbers and skill levels.

Here is an ideal model for a full-time guitar teacher. The guitar teacher teaches six classes of guitar in a middle school. In a perfect world, there would be three beginning guitar classes, two intermediate guitar classes, and one advanced guitar class. Each class would have thirty or more students for a total of about 180 students. As mentioned, this is an ideal situation that may not apply to you, but even this perfect situation could go badly if not professionally managed.

Let's assume that the advanced class of thirty students is made up of all eighth graders who will be leaving the school at the end of the year—as is most likely the case. If there are 180 students, when the eighth graders in the advanced class leave, there will only be 150 students left. The math looks like this: 180 – 30 = 150. Yet there are also most likely eighth graders in all of your classes, including the beginning and intermediate classes. There could be another group of thirty eighth graders from those classes. Now, the math looks like this: 150 – 30 = 120.

Figuring out the number of eighth graders leaving is as easy as looking at the class roster or grade book, but the next number is going to be a guess at best. A certain number of students are going to move away, change schools, or change electives. The best guest is there will be another group of thirty students who will make these changes. The math now looks like this: 120 – 30 = 90.

We started with a total of 180 students and are now down to just ninety. (Generally speaking, it is safe to assume that your program will have a 50 percent retention rate. Some programs will have a higher rate, but the average will be around 50 percent.) Of these remaining ninety students, there will be no eighth graders, and a large percentage of the other students who have left the program are likely to have been low-performance students or students who simply did not enjoy learning to play the guitar. You might then assume that the remaining ninety students will fill two intermediate classes with a total of sixty students, and one advanced class of thirty. All of the seats in the three beginning guitar classes are now empty. To keep the numbers the same as the previous year, you will need ninety new beginner students.

In this model, we have answered the simple question of how many students will be needed to fill the total number of empty seats for six classes, but projections become more complex when you consider skill level and class distribution. Every teacher should have a number in mind of what it will take not only to maintain the status quo, but also to keep like-skilled students together in the same class and avoid classes of mixed skill levels. This particular model may have provided the math to estimate the required number of students in each class to meet class size requirements for the program, but there could be a weakness in this model: that is, although the number of students was met, the skill level of the students may not be aligned. You may have thirty students in each of your intermediate classes, but with a vast range of skills. What is missing?

A simple method is to tie class placement to quarter grades. For example, in order for a beginning guitar student to advance to the intermediate level, each student must have a B or better for all four quarters and attend all required rehearsals and performances. The same could be true for intermediate students wishing to be promoted to the advanced class.

Setting this requirement means that the mixed levels of skill should not be as big a problem. School counselors should also adhere to this procedure to avoid placing students incorrectly. For students new to the school, there should be a required audition that reflects skills needed to successfully be in the intermediate class or the advanced class. Otherwise, all new students to the school are automatically placed into a beginning guitar class, which may not always be appropriate. Grade level should not be a consideration when it comes to class placement. In other words, an eighth grader should not be placed in the advanced guitar class, because the student is in the eighth grade. A student should be placed in advanced guitar after having completed beginning guitar with a B or better and completed intermediate guitar with a B or better. The exception is if a student new to the school auditions and demonstrates the same skills required for the intermediate or the advanced classes.

Rewards for Longevity

Many high school students join the guitar program as freshmen. They know that the longer they stay in the program, the more they will learn. That is of course the whole idea of a music program, but it may not be enough of a reason for students to stay in the program. When organizing a program, be sure to design rewards for student longevity. Let us look at an example for a high school guitar program, which may be altered to fit any program. Because grade level does not necessarily correspond to how long a student has been in the program, we will be using "year-one students," "year-two students," etc.

Year-one students

- are assigned guitars destined as first-year guitars. These are the oldest and least expensive guitars in the inventory.

- will be placed in the beginning guitar ensemble
- wear coordinated T-shirts or polo shirts to all public performances
- perform only one performance at the end of the school year

Year-two students

- are assigned nicer, newer guitars
- wear coordinated performance uniforms different from that of the year-one students
- are eligible to audition for the intermediate guitar ensemble
- are eligible to audition to perform in the Fall Recital
- will perform on all large-ensemble performances during the school year
- are eligible to participate in the Solo and Ensemble Festival
- will participate in the district ensemble festival
- are eligible to audition for honor guitar ensemble

Year-three students

- can do everything year-two students can do
- wear coordinated performance uniform different from those of the year-one and year-two students
- be eligible for travel
- may audition for the advanced guitar ensemble
- may be eligible to hold an office within their ensemble

Year-four students

- can do everything year-three students can do
- wear coordinated performance uniforms different from those of year-one through year-three students
- are assigned designated senior guitars. These are the newest, most expensive instruments in the inventory.
- are eligible to audition to be in the Senior Guitar Quartet, the highest honor of the entire guitar program
- are expected to perform in the Senior Recital
- will choose all of the music for the final concert of the year, called Seniors' Choice

- will have an awards night at which outstanding senior guitar students receive various awards for their four years of participation

On the basis of this model, students have something new to look forward to each year. Students feel, for instance, that they are progressing because they are playing on better instruments, doing more performances, wearing nicer performance uniforms, and being more active and engaged. Depending on your situation, there may be many more privileges to add to this list. Think about how each level can feel like an advancement. In this model, fourth-year students have the most opportunities, often a factor when an eligible high school student starts thinking about graduating a year early. Do they want to miss their senior year and all of the perks and activities that go with that?

Practical Ideas for How to Motivate Students

Do you ever wonder what it would take to convince students to do something you would really like them to do? The first big step in the process is to have a clear definition of what you would like your students to accomplish. The second step is to decide to what degree you are willing to go to reward such accomplishments. Here are a few real examples of rewards and accomplishments.

The Double Century Club

Desire: You want students to score well on weekly playing tests. Students are given two playing tests every other week. What would it take to motivate a student to receive two perfect scores?

Reward: Create the "Double Century Club." This is not a real club. There are no meetings, no dues, and absolutely no elements that resemble a club. And yet students will want to be in the club in the worst way. How does one have acceptance in the club? Students who receive two perfect consecutive scores—two consecutive 100s on playing tests—receive admission into the club for a two-week period. If they want to be back in the club after two weeks, they must score another set of perfect scores. The maximum number of times a student can be in the Double Century Club during the school year is sixteen times. Over the years, a number of my students have been in the club ten or more times. And yes, some students made it in the club all sixteen times in a single year. Is this effective? Yes. Are there costs involved? No!

The Guitar Letter or Guitar Patch

Desire: You want students to participate in both honor guitar and solo and ensemble and to attend all rehearsals and performances.

Reward: Create a Guitar Letter or a Guitar Patch. This patch may be sewn onto a jacket, sweater, or hat, or may be framed. A student may earn one patch per school year. The requirements may include almost anything. Our model includes auditioning for honor guitar (regardless if student makes it or not), participating in solo and ensemble (regardless if students do well or not), and attending all required after-school rehearsals and performances. This award was another major motivator for my students who wanted to collect a patch for all four years of guitar while in high school. Is this effective? Yes. Are there costs involved? Each patch costs about five dollars.

The Graduation Music Cord

Desire: You want to encourage guitar students to take other music classes, including music theory, piano, and one other music class of their choice, usually music technology. Or for their third class, they could choose from choir, band, jazz band, guitar quartet, chamber class, orchestra, mariachi, or handbells.

Reward: Create a music cord for students to wear at graduation. Students who complete three music classes as well as guitar class receive a music cord to wear over their gown during graduation. Because this task takes at least three years to accomplish, it is planned during the freshman year and makes the guitar students more well-rounded musicians. Is this effective? Yes. Are there costs involved? Each cord costs about eight dollars.

Wall of Fame

Desire: You want students to strive for excellence over a long period of time.

Reward: Create awards that students may strive to accomplish only during their senior year. Develop a Wall of Fame with attractive, high-quality, professional perpetual plaques (one that holds up to twelve names for a period of twelve years) on which student names may be engraved during their senior year if they are selected for that particular award. For example, the Guitarist of the Year Award may be one of the perpetual plaques that hang in a prominent location in the classroom. Students and visitors may walk into the room and immediately see which students were selected for each year for this very prestigious award. A senior student's name and the year may be engraved each year.

Other awards may include Most Improved Award, Most Versatile Award, Most Likely to Become a Music Educator Award, Principal's Award, Director's Award, Best Rock Guitarist of the Year, and Best Classical Guitarist of the Year. Be creative and have as many as you can afford on one designated wall.

Are perpetual awards effective? Yes! Are there any costs involved? Yes. Each plaque costs about a hundred dollars but is good for twelve years.

A Real-Life Example

Note that the following real-life example as well as those later in the chapter are contributions by Douglas Back, who taught at Carver Elementary Arts Magnet School in Montgomery, Alabama. These ideas first appeared in print in the Guitar Foundation of America's *Soundboard* in the Fall issue, 1995, and are being used here with permission from the author.

Douglas Back created a *Wall of Fame* in his classroom. He divided his entire curriculum into ten levels similarly to the Royal Conservatory of Music in Toronto and Trinity College London. When a student completes the first five levels, their name goes on the board. If a student completes all ten levels before graduating, their 11" × 14" photo is framed and goes on the wall permanently under the title Young Virtuoso Club. To date, only three students have made it in the Young Virtuoso Club. This means it is possible, just not easy, and not everyone can or will do it. Is this effective? According to Back, this was quite inspirational for a handful of students. Are there any costs involved? Yes, but minimally.[*]

[*] Douglas Back, "Creative Teaching Techniques with Young Students and a Profile of a Guitar Program in an Elementary Arts School," *Soundboard: The Journal of the Guitar Foundation of America* (Fall 1995), 27–33

Officer Positions

Desire: You want students to take a leadership role within the ensemble or class and have a say in the shaping of the class.

Reward: Create officer positions such as president, vice president, secretary, and treasurer and have students run for these positions. They will be elected by peer voting. Once students are in place with office roles, meet with these leaders regularly and have them be the liaisons between you and each class. Encourage the class leaders to contribute to such responsibilities as ensemble selection, uniforms, trips, performance ideas, and fundraising. Whatever is on the table, allow these leaders to have a say in shaping what happens in the classroom. Is this effective? Yes! Are there any costs involved? None.

Guitar Karate Belts

Desire: You want students to complete various requirements for skill levels.

Reward: Elementary teachers for years have used Karate Belts, which are colored cords that tie on the bell of a recorder. When students learning recorder pass a certain skill level, they receive a colored cord. The goal is to fill the bell of the recorder with all nine cords. Each cord becomes a little more difficult to earn. These cords are now available for ukulele and guitar and are very reasonably priced. It is just a matter of defining what skills the students must meet to receive each colored cord. Is this effective? Yes! Are there any costs involved? Yes. Actual cords are available for purchase on the Internet and you can easily find them at retailers like Musick8.com via an online search. Some teachers use colored stickers to indicate belt level.

Real-Life Examples

Douglas Back modified the idea of Karate Belts for guitar in his classroom. Instead of using colored cords as rewards, he found a stencil cutter in the shape of a guitar and cut out guitars in various colored construction paper. He then hole-punched the top of the guitar and added a ribbon that can be tied to a guitar. These rewards were used in place of a colored cord.

Were they effective? According to Back, very much so. Are there any costs involved? Yes, but minimally.

Back also wanted his students to become well-rounded guitarists. To inspire them, he created an annual event that he referred to as a Guitar Olympics. This annual event has five categories of competition and each student is encouraged to participate in every category. The first category is the Solo Selection Event in which each student selects a level-appropriate piece, memorizes it, and performs for a judge. The top three highest-scoring performers are recognized with a certificate. The Two Octave Scale event is playing a designated two-octave scale with the proper left- and right-hand fingerings as quickly and accurately as possible. The Sight-Reading Event is a competition to identify the top three best sight-readers. The Speed Demon Event is a competition to determine which top three students can perform "The Irish Washerwoman" at the fastest tempo and most accurately. The Fingerboard Spelling Event is a written and timed exam to see who the top three scoring students are who can identify and name notes and finger positions. Are there any costs involved? It depends on who the judges are and if they are being paid. Otherwise, just the cost of the paper certificates for each of the top three winners in each of the five categories.[*]

[*] Back, "Creative Teaching Techniques."

Chair Positions

Desire: You want students to learn their parts in ensemble music.

Reward: Borrowing from band and orchestra programs, students in a section of the ensemble may compete for the first-chair position. Some teachers have regular auditions for chair placement. Others allow students to challenge students sitting ahead of them in the section for chair placement. A challenge becomes a competition among students to demonstrate how well each student can play their assigned parts in the ensemble. The winner either retains the current chair or gets to move up in the section, depending on current placement. Is this effective? Yes! Are there any costs involved? No.

6

Selecting Your Instrument and Approach

At one time in the United States, no public schools anywhere offered music classes in guitar. One of the earliest public-school guitar classes was taught by Dave Mortland and offered at Webster Groves High School in Missouri in 1964. Mortland gave classroom instruction to students who were interested in learning to play the guitar, and his students performed as an ensemble. At the time, students were encouraged to bring guitars from home. For students who did not have a family instrument, a local music store owned by the well-known music author and publisher Mel Bay provided guitars. Bay would also frequently visit this guitar classroom to assist Mortland with teaching.[1]

Since then, guitar education has undergone significant development and growth in the United States, and many of the lessons learned from the early days still resonate with current guitar educators. This chapter will provide a brief overview of the history of the guitar and classroom guitar education in the United States, and consider how contemporary guitar educators can make informed decisions about instrument selection and pedagogical approaches for their program.

Classical Guitar in the Classroom

Guitar education in the United States has an interesting history. Mortland and Bay's 1964 experiment in public-school guitar education had been long in the making. In 1954, Bay was invited to speak at the Music Educators National Conference in Washington, DC. By then, he had already published what would be his bestselling *Modern Guitar Method*. During his presentation, Bay shared his dream that guitar would be taught in public schools across the country. These comments prompted objections from an audience member, who suggested there would be a man on the moon before guitar was ever taught in public schools. Motivated by this comment, Bay began to work

Building an Award-Winning Guitar Program. Bill Swick, Oxford University Press. © Oxford University Press 2022.
DOI: 10.1093/oso/9780197609804.003.0006

toward creating the first public-school guitar class. It took ten years, but his efforts became a reality at Webster Groves High School—and it happened five years before the first man landed on the moon!

Just a few years later, in 1968, Jerry Snyder began teaching his first guitar class at Piedmont High School in San Jose, California. Acoustic steel-string guitars, which were very popular and readily available at most music stores, were what most students brought to school (as with Webster Groves, the school did not provide instruments). In my personal correspondence with Jerry, he recalled that seventy students signed up for the first year; students brought what they had, including electric guitars that he would plug into amplification only on Fridays.[2]

In 1969, Snyder helped a total of ten high schools start guitar programs in the San Jose area. The schools collectively applied for and received grant money to purchase enough nylon-string guitars for all of the schools. The point to this story is there was a need to have all of one kind of guitar. It was decided at the time that nylon-string guitars were the best choice because the strings are easier on the fingers, the guitars tend to blend well together, and their price can be less expensive. When you are purchasing a large number of guitars, cost can be a major factor.

These ten schools would eventually become models for future schools, not only in California but in other parts of the country as well.

In the 1970s and 1980s, when public schools began to consider offering guitar class for credit, they first needed approval from their respective states' board of education. The easiest way to get a new class approved was to find a school that had already been approved to offer guitar and copy everything about that school's program. As more schools began offering guitar classes based on the San Jose models, particularly in states that did not yet have the programs, those schools would then become models in their own states, and so on. Because the first models provided nylon-string guitars, so did those that copied the programs.

During the mid-1960s and early 1970s, highly skilled classical guitarists were also starting to offer private guitar lessons in a small number of select universities. Students wishing to study guitar at one of these universities were expected to own and learn to play a nylon-string guitar. Many of these early teachers were guitarists from Europe or had gone to Europe to study guitar, and the pedagogy of this time was heavily influenced by the Spanish traditions of guitar playing.

Gut, Nylon, and Steel: A Brief History of Guitar Strings

For better understanding of the term classical guitar, it helps to know a bit of music history. During the Renaissance period, there was a much smaller stringed instrument with four sets of doubled strings (a total of eight strings) known as the Renaissance guitar, along with larger instruments of five or even six courses (strings in combinations of single and double strings).[3] Later, during the Baroque period, the four-course guitar grew somewhat larger and had either five sets of double strings (a total or ten strings) or just five single strings (Figure 6.1). This instrument is known as the Baroque guitar. In the Classical period, the guitar grew larger still and a sixth string was added to create the instrument now known as the classical guitar (Figure 6.2).

During the Romantic period, the guitar as an instrument did not undergo many changes, yet the technique of playing the classical guitar changed significantly during the Romantic period. Romantic guitarists like Francisco Tarrega experimented with plucking the strings with fingernails, avoiding playing melodies on open strings, and playing farther down the neck on lower strings to create warmer, more expressive tones. The Romantic guitarists began to improve the sound of the guitar through the art of playing and by applying new techniques, such as the inclusion of ponticello and tasto. More attention was given to dynamics, tonal color, and the emphasis of moving voices than before. Though the new Romantic techniques (still being used today) have improved the overall sound of the guitar, luthiers continue

Figure 6.1 Baroque guitar

Figure 6.2 Classical guitar

to experiment with the instrument to create more volume and a wider range of tones. Despite these internal alterations, the body size and string length of the modern classical guitar are still quite similar to the original design of the guitar of the Classical period.

A full history of the guitar and its design is out of scope for this book, but for those who are interested, I would recommend the work of British historian and author Christopher Page. Page is an expert on medieval music, instruments, and performance practice, as well as the social and musical history of the guitar in England from the sixteenth to the nineteenth centuries. His writings capture the importance of the guitar to humans over three centuries and how humans respond in a different way to the guitar from how they do to other instruments. Page's work celebrates the rich history of the guitar's development, which can help you to more effectively teach your students to appreciate the instrument, its music, and its past.[4] In addition to his books, Page has a number of YouTube lectures that are both informative and entertaining. Here are a couple of links to Page's lectures. The first is "The Guitar and the Romantic Vision of the Medieval World" (https:// youtu.be/y0ndu1YP2sE). The next is "The Guitar in the Age of Charles I" (https://youtu.be/7prn-miW-bI). Both are far more entertaining than the titles may suggests and include performances of period instruments.

The important thing to note is that in this book, when we refer to classical guitars or nylon-string guitars, we are referring to an instrument design (size, shape, etc.) that comes out of the Classical period rather than a particular style of playing or genre of music.

The original guitars during the early periods used gut strings. As suggested by the name, these strings were typically made from the intestines of either pigs, goats, or sheep—or in some cases, larger animals. (Though these strings are often also called "catgut strings," the intestines of cats were not typically used.) The practice of making strings from animal intestines continues today, but largely for the purposes of historical performance. That is, musicians who perform early music on early instruments might prefer the sound of catgut strings and favor the historical correctness of this instrument design. In fact, it was not until 1947 that nylon strings began to replace catgut strings. During the unrest in Europe leading to World War II, there was a shortage of gut strings. Albert Augustine, a New York guitar maker, went to DuPont shortly after the end of World War II and was able to obtain a supply of their newly developed nylon threads. Augustine then built a machine capable of shaping these nylon threads into the diameters and lengths needed to create guitar strings. World-renowned classical guitarist Andres Segovia endorsed these strings, and his photo is still being used today on the packaging of Augustine strings (Figure 6.3).[5] To hear a comparison of gut strings and nylon strings played on the same guitar by the same player,

Figure 6.3 Augustine String packaging

view "Introducing: Gut Strings on the Classical Guitar" by Brandon Acker on YouTube (https://www.youtube.com/watch?v=kFZVg8EK88I).

In 1922, following the end of World War I, the first commercial steel strings were made available for sale to the US public. Steel strings were used in Europe, but they were extremely expensive. Technology from World War I taught the United States how to manufacture steel much more cheaply. With cheap steel, steel strings were affordable. World War II was responsible for the development of plastics, and it was after WWII that nylon strings were first manufactured. There were no manufacturers of gut strings in the United States, so the strings were very expensive, were imported from Europe, were often not made well (making for poor intonation), and broke easily. The idea of having a string that does not easily break (steel) and was both available and affordable made steel strings attractive.

Many guitar owners purchased steel strings and put them on their guitars, without realizing one very important problem. The standard pressure created by a full set of gut strings was about sixty pounds, the amount of pressure that most guitars built before the 1920s were constructed and designed to withstand on the body, bridge, and neck. The early sets of steel strings, on the other hand, created about six hundred pounds of pressure—ten times the amount the classical guitar was constructed to handle. In just a few years, thousands of guitars were ruined and deemed unplayable because of the damage that the excessive pressure of steel strings created.[6]

Once steel strings had become available to the public, the guitar manufacturers C. F. Martin & Co. began adjusting the internal bracings of their guitars and created a new guitar model that was sold in 1922, intended specifically for the use of steel strings. Martin then began building newly designed guitars in the 1930s. These instruments have larger bodies, have longer necks with fourteen frets (rather than the twelve of classical guitars), and are braced differently to withstand the added pressure of steel strings; the necks are reinforced with an adjustable steel rod. Known as Dreadnoughts, these guitars are the model we refer to today as acoustic guitars or steel-string guitars. Many manufacturers have created variations of this style of guitar, but Martin was the first to build a Dreadnought (apparently named after the contemporaneous British battleship),[7] designed to withstand the added pressure of steel strings.

While Martin was building Dreadnought guitars, Gibson Mandolin-Guitar Manufacturing Company and other guitar manufacturers began manufacturing archtop acoustic guitars that were also engineered to use steel strings. These instruments were quite popular for playing jazz, swing, and country music, and eventually led to the addition of magnetic pickups for amplification. It was the development of steel strings that allowed the magnetic pickup to work.

If you google "steel string guitars versus nylon-sting guitars" you will find dozens and dozens of opinions and articles about how the two differ and which one is better for which purpose. You could say these two instruments are different tools designed for different purposes, like different types of hammers or screwdrivers. Simply put, you would select an acoustic steel-string guitar to strum chords and play with a pick. Nylon-string guitars are used more frequently for fingerpicking styles and/or classical music. Though there are always exceptions, generally speaking, steel-string guitars tend to be used more frequently for playing country music, rock, popular music, bluegrass, and Gypsy jazz. Nylon-string guitars are used to perform classical music, finger-style music, Latin music, flamenco, mariachi, and smooth jazz.

Classical versus Popular Music

Classroom guitar teachers often fall along a spectrum when it comes to teaching styles of music: classical versus popular. These styles tend to be associated with different instruments and string types. Some teachers believe that classroom guitar should be taught strictly in the classical fashion by using classical posture and classical technique, and performing music from the standard classical repertoire; students are taught to play only on nylon-string guitars, pluck the strings by using fingerpicking style, and read only modern Western staff notation. Other teachers favor acoustic steel-string guitars and a pedagogy focused on popular music repertoire. These teachers might teach students to use guitar picks, strum chords, and read music written in modern tablature.

There are some major differences between these two camps; in fact, it is difficult to believe that two models can be so different and yet be referred to by the same name. When asked, many music educators teaching guitar will claim that they fall somewhere in the middle. In a recent survey sent to music educators in every state in the United States who teach one or more guitar classes, 49 percent of the teachers responded that their classroom is outfitted with nylon-string guitars. Thirty-seven percent responded that they use steel-string guitars in the classroom. Only 14 percent of the programs use a mix of the two. When it came to genre and style, 39 percent of the teachers indicated that they teach strictly classical guitar. The same number of teachers, 39 percent, responded that they teach popular and folk music. Twenty-two percent responded that they have a mixture of both. Thirty-two percent of those who took the survey majored in guitar while they were in college. Sixty-eight percent of the teachers indicated that the guitar is a secondary instrument.

These are real numbers representing music educators from every state in the union. The numbers indicate that the two camps, classical versus popular, are perfectly balanced, with equal numbers of teachers teaching classical versus popular and folk music. This data also shows that respondents collectively prefer nylon strings over steel strings, though only by 25 percent. Yet when we look at the breakdown of responses based on the teachers' educational background, we find that a striking 100 percent of the teachers taking the survey who majored in guitar in college teach on nylon-string guitars. Of the teachers who did not study guitar in college, 61 percent prefer steel-string guitars.[8]

This data seems to indicate that teachers who have had strong training in guitar in college (and have thus dedicated a large portion of their lives to learning to play the guitar) tend to favor classical guitar. On the other side, a slight majority of music educators who are teaching guitar as a secondary instrument tend to favor steel-string instruments and popular music.

This discussion is not meant to settle a debate about which method or approach is objectively better, though this book favors the use of nylon-string guitars and I give some reasons for my preference in the next section. When making the decision for your own classroom, think about the purpose of your program. Are you building a program with a goal of assisting students getting into college as music majors? Or are you teaching the guitar as an elective class? I recommend that those focusing on building a program think seriously about which guitars to use, weighing all the factors. For instance, will steel-string guitar students be able to participate in ensemble events? Will your repertoire and pedagogy align with state standards? Can your program and students afford more expensive instruments? With these kinds of questions in mind, guitar teachers can find it easy to go with nylon-string instruments. If you are teaching just one or two classes, then you have a bit more freedom in using whatever is available.

One caveat about genre and style: as popular music education becomes more common, programs like Little Kids Rock or School of Rock focus on high-level instruction of commercial music. Generally, these classes include additional instruments rather than only guitar, and do not fall under the state standards for guitar class. Yet this general point in no way suggests that teaching popular music is a bad thing. Guitar classes should include exposure to many genres, including popular music. Popular music is not the issue; the point here is to make sure you are teaching the content as outlined in the state standards.

Twelve Reasons for Using Classical Nylon-String Guitars in the Classroom

Again, there are many debates and personal preferences when it comes to using classical nylon-string guitars or acoustic steel-string guitars in the classroom. Though arguments can be made on both sides, I would recommend nylon-string guitars for most school guitar programs for the following reasons:

1. More than four centuries of history of the catgut string guitar have produced both a tradition and a host of method books still being used today. Many of the effective guitar method books today have been influenced by the past centuries of European repertoire and technique.

2. All university programs from the 1960s through the 1980s were first modeled after the work of Andres Segovia, a world-renowned classical guitar virtuoso, and require guitar majors to study and perform on a classical nylon-string guitar. Any students graduating from secondary schools who wish to major in guitar while they are in college will be better prepared from having learned to play on a nylon-string guitar, provided they are exposed to the standard guitar repertoire.

3. Universally, the word "guitar" refers to a Classical-period nylon-string guitar. All other guitars require an adjective: for example, solid-body electric guitar, acoustic guitar, steel-string guitar, arch-top guitar, jazz guitar, semi-hollow guitar.

4. Various cultures and styles of guitar playing such as flamenco, calypso, tango, mariachi, reggae, and jota also use nylon-string guitars. This use makes it easier to teach a variety of genres outside of Western popular music.

5. The classical nylon-string guitar has an ever-growing repertoire of both solo and ensemble music, as well as concerto repertoire, much of which is very contemporary in style. The vast amount of literature written for classical guitar continues to expand year after year, providing a wide choice of music written in many genres.

6. The nylon-string guitar has a slightly smaller body than that of an acoustic steel-string guitar. The classical guitar is thus more accessible for smaller students.

7. The nylon strings are softer on the fingers of the left hand, and are thus easier to play, especially for beginner students.

8. Nylon-string guitars are constructed with wider necks, with more space between the strings, so that the right hand has room for fingerpicking. This is possibly the greatest argument. State curriculum requires inclusion of both left-hand and right-hand technique.

   It is difficult to teach right-hand technique on an instrument on which the strings are not spaced for the right hand. The nylon-string guitar is designed with the correct spacing.

9. It is easier to play an acoustic steel-string or an electric guitar after learning to play on a nylon-string guitar. The same is not true in reverse. In Kenneth Peres's article, *Will Playing Classical Guitar Make Playing Electric Guitar Easier?*, Peres refers to guitarist Paul Gilbert as a demigod of rock-guitar shred. Peres mentions that Gilbert spends most of his practice time in playing classical nylon-string guitars and explains that the wider neck, higher action, and thicker strings make playing a steel-string electric guitar far easier. Ken Hower, an acquaintance of Gilbert, confirms that Gilbert practices on nylon-string guitars. Many well-known electric guitarists have mentioned that they do most of their practicing on nylon-string guitars to increase their speed when switching to an electric.[8]

10. Nylon-string guitars are generally less expensive than acoustic or electric guitars. Nylon-string guitars are still available in the $100 price range for programs starting on a tight budget.

11. Nylon-string guitars have a warmer tone and tend to blend together very well in a large ensemble.

12. Most state music-education conferences require nylon-string guitars to participate in solo and ensemble festivals and all-state ensembles. The NAfME All National Honor Guitar Ensemble, for example, requires nylon-string guitars.

All these reasons do not mean that you cannot teach steel-string guitars in the classroom. However, doing so may limit what you can teach as well as opportunities for your students while they are in your program and afterwards.

Beginning Pedagogy

All students enrolled in a public-school guitar class should be taught to read music from modern staff notation. Guitar class should be no different from public-school band or orchestra. This philosophy is also practical, because many solo and ensemble organizations (discussed in greater detail in Chapter 7) may require that students perform from modern staff notation rather than other kinds of written music. Instrumental classes for credit to graduate from public school should follow the national standards set by the NAfME, which have been adopted by each State Department of Education as state standards. The only exception is the state of Texas, which has its own strict guidelines.

The standards for Year One, or Beginning Guitar, include teaching music by standard staff notation and teaching the placement of eighteen notes in first position on all six strings. This requirement has nothing to do with classical style, pop style, or any other genre of music. It involves teaching note reading and note placement, much as you would do for a beginning band or orchestra class.

Ideally, students will be able to play in first position by the middle of the first year. The second half of the year may be spent in playing simple melodies and ensemble arrangements written in first position.

The NAfME Best Practices for Guitar provides a list of skills that should be taught during the first year of guitar in order to meet state and national standards. This document also outlines all of the skills that should be included for four levels of guitar classes. (See Appendix B, "Best Practices for Guitar Education.")

Teaching Classical Music at the Intermediate Level

If the guitar teacher is following the state standards, all students at the second-year level—also referred to as the intermediate level—will be able to play all of the notes in first position in the keys of C major, A minor, F major, D minor, G major, and E minor.

Though there are no method books in print that promote this next idea, just know that it is very effective and has been tested in many classrooms since 2000. Before introducing solo classical guitar to students, consider introducing the literature of classical guitar first through ensemble playing.

Here is the concept. Students are introduced to the works of the Baroque composer Fernando Sor (c. 1778–1839) in class. Before playing his music there may be a discussion about Sor's significance, including what countries he lived in, how prolific he was as a composer, and with what musical period he is most strongly associated. In this discussion of Sor's life it would be important to point out that he studied composition from the Neapolitan composer Federico Moretti (1769–1839), who taught him to write by using three independent voices. This information is important because much of Sor's music can be arranged for three parts quite easily and intermediate-level students can play and hear Sor's music through the experience of ensemble playing. Directors may find ample three-part arrangements of Fernando Sor's music at JWPepper.com and Guitarintheclassroom.com.

After this introduction, the director may distribute parts of an ensemble arrangement of one of Sor's compositions and students may experience the music by each playing only one of the three parts. This is a way to expose students to the literature of classical guitar music without having the skills to play these pieces on solo guitar.

Students who continue to study guitar will eventually have the skills to play multivoiced parts on the guitar: that is, two or more voices at the same time. Having some familiarity with the music, and knowing the melodies and tempos, will greatly assist students in transitioning from playing a single part in a guitar ensemble arrangement to playing all of the parts simultaneously. The idea of using ensemble arrangements to prepare students to play the same material as solo pieces really works.

Solo Playing versus Ensemble Playing

Many music educators have looked at how piano has been taught in a group/classroom setting and tried to duplicate that model for guitar. Such a model includes what many music colleges have had for decades: electric piano labs in which students can enroll and learn basic skills on the piano. Everyone in the class has their own piano keyboard and wears headphones to be able to hear only themselves while playing. In these labs, the teachers have a control panel that enables them to listen to each student individually and speak to individual students to give instructions. These can be like mini private lessons even though there are multiple students in one class, because each student is playing at a different level and working on different pages of a method book.

When the idea of teaching guitar as a class was first discussed, many assumed that a guitar class would look and function like a piano lab. In other words, students would enter the class at various skill levels and the teacher would work with each student privately. In this model, guitar students would use method books that direct them to play the guitar in the classical style as a solo instrument.

Other music educators, however, instantly saw parallels between the orchestra model and guitar class. Students could learn the guitar together while they are working on the same page from the same method book and learning to read music and count rhythms. Eventually, the guitar class could perform as an ensemble just as a beginning string orchestra class would. In this model, there is no solo-playing component.

As guitar classes started developing, both models have been used, and it has more or less been one model or the other; the two are rarely mixed. I suggest instead that to build an award-winning guitar program, you can blend these two models in your teaching. Diving into the specifics of guitar pedagogy, however, is out of the scope of this book. If these topics are of interest, I cover them in my book *Teaching Beginning Guitar Class*.[9] The purpose of this section is merely to highlight how important it is to teach both ensemble and solo playing. Students must learn collectively and experience being a part of a large ensemble, but they should also learn the skills of solo playing individually. Both are important aspects of guitar education and student development and should be considered for inclusion of any award-winning program.

7

Solo and Ensemble and Other Festivals

Most music educators are familiar with the term solo and ensemble, generally used to reference a festival or a competition. As the name suggests, in these events students may register to perform a solo and/or perform with a small ensemble and be adjudicated. Many states will have a solo and ensemble organization in place through the state MEA. The competition begins at the local or district level, moves up to the regional level, and culminates at the state level. Solo and ensemble competitions have been available for decades for band, choir, and orchestra, and directors know that participating in these events can be an important step toward building an award-winning program. The same is true for your guitar program. The question is if guitar has been accepted in your area or state. This chapter covers the basics of preparing for solo and ensemble and other festivals, and how to advocate for opportunities for your students.

Preparing for Solo and Ensemble Festivals

An award-winning guitar program will prepare students to perform solo as well as in an ensemble. Beginning students should be encouraged to perform with small ensembles. Playing with others helps combat the nerves, and the group can provide a sense of confidence that an individual student may not find when performing solo. As students get older and gain experience performing, they will also be better prepared to participate as a soloist. A well-balanced guitar program, for instance, might have its upperclassmen (juniors and seniors) prepare to perform solo materials on a classical, nylon-string guitar while students from year two to year four are preparing to perform in small ensembles. Each festival has rules and guidelines that are generally made public to all music educators in the area. There are usually limits to how many ensembles one student may participate in.

If your guitar program is new and your students are not ready to participate in the solo division, begin with small ensembles. The categories for small

Building an Award-Winning Guitar Program. Bill Swick, Oxford University Press. © Oxford University Press 2022.
DOI: 10.1093/oso/9780197609804.003.0007

ensembles are generally duos, trios, and quartets (some festivals will allow larger ensembles; some will not). If yours is a new guitar program participating in a solo and ensemble festival for the first time, I recommend that you enter the trio category. This suggestion is strategic. Ensemble repertoire has ample materials for duos and quartets, yet it is not the same for trios. While more composers are now writing or arranging for trios, the trio area is still behind in terms of performance material. The result is that there is generally less competition in this area, and your students will likely have a more positive experience by entering into this category. To get some ideas for repertoire, go to YouTube and search "guitar trio classical," and you will find plenty of resources to consider.

The first question you might ask yourself is what repertoire is accepted for a solo and ensemble festival. A good place to start is with the University of Texas University Interscholastic League (UIL) Prescribed Music List, which can be found at www.uiltexas.org/pml/. This list has been the go-to list for many years for music educators both teaching in and outside of Texas. These selections are graded one (hardest) through six (easiest). The Texas UIL list, however, does not offer selections for guitar in grades four, five, or six; the easiest selections for guitar will be level three. In searching for music in the Texas UIL list, you will find it helpful to know the codes. Guitar Quartet is code 444, Guitar Trio is code 434, and Acoustic Guitar Solo is code 405.

In the state of Texas, to advance to the next level a student must perform a grade-one selection and receive a top rating. Grade-one selections on the UIL Prescribed Music List are quite challenging and are geared for students who have studied the classical guitar seriously with a private teacher and/or have attended a school with a significant guitar program that teaches classical technique from the beginning. This type of school will likely have an extensive library of classical guitar literature. In other words, grade-one selections are most likely to be performed by students who belong to established and well-resourced guitar programs.

Happily, unless you live in the state of Texas, chances are the guidelines will not be as strict in your region. Your state may not have any guidelines for guitar literature for solo and ensemble. In these cases especially, referencing the Texas UIL Prescribed Music List is a good place to start to get an idea what the ultimate goal may be.

One thing to be mindful of is that not all pieces in the same grade are equal. Some titles in the grade-one category are easier than others, for example, and this is one instance in which having a knowledge of the repertoire comes in handy. If you are lacking in this area, it is easy to find almost every title on the UIL list on YouTube. Take the time to do the work and become familiar with the music on the Texas UIL list. It will help you and your students to know which pieces are more or less challenging, even though they may count for the same grade level.

Knowing the UIL list well will also help you understand the guitar repertoire considered to be at playing level for a precollege guitar student so that you can better help your students prepare for auditions. Selecting music is a major part of any competition, audition, or performance. Can the students play this music with ease, with expression, and with musical command? Do the students "own" the piece in terms of being in absolute control? Finding the right pieces to match your students' skill level is a major task.

If and when there is funding to purchase music, the Texas UIL list, then, is a particularly good resource. All pieces listed include the publishers' names, which make it easy to find. Purchase music from all grades available. Expose students to this music by starting with the easiest grade (for guitar, this is grade three) and working up to grade one. Be sure, if you have the funding, to purchase music for soloists, trios, and quartets. In theory, there is often a greater need for solo music because these pieces will be one per student, but as mentioned earlier, for beginning programs with students participating for the very first time, playing in an ensemble may be a better first experience than playing as a soloist.

Finally, though we've used the term competition several times in this chapter already, remember that solo and ensemble festivals are usually *not* competitions against other students or schools, but rather an opportunity for students to play in front of an adjudicator for a score. Every student is rewarded for participating, usually by receiving a colored medal that correlates to their score. In many festivals blue represents the highest score, then red, white, and finally a red, white, and blue metal (arguably the most attractive of the four medals).

Once the event is over, do not be shy to publicize how well your students have done at a solo and ensemble festival. Promote the successes of all your students and make an effort to recognize every participant for their accomplishments. For an award-winning program, it is important to learn to call attention to student achievements. Publicize the event on your website; include information about the medals your students won in the program for the next concert; contact the administrator in charge of student activities and share details along with photos of the students displaying their medals.

Make certain your supervising administrator is made aware of your students' accomplishments, as well as the school principal. In addition, contact the faculty member who oversees the school newspaper and yearbook. Students should be proud of their participation in festivals and you should advocate for their recognition.

Knowing the Guidelines

While appropriate music selection is extremely important, directors must know other key guidelines to help their students succeed at solo and ensemble festivals.

It's useful to know, for example, that nylon-string guitars tend to be the standard for solo and ensemble festivals. Some festivals are even extremely specific about nylon-string guitars only. Other festivals have no guidelines, but the adjudicators may have the power to eliminate or lower scores for ensembles that perform on steel-string instruments while playing music written for nylon strings. It goes without saying that you should always perform the repertoire on the instrument for which it was written. If the guidelines for using one type of guitar or another are not clear in your area, push for clarity. You don't want your students to miss out or lose points because of their instrument selection.

Most solo and ensemble festivals do not require memorization at the first level, and students may bring music to read. The standard for participating in a solo and ensemble festival is reading from modern staff notation. While some teachers may disagree philosophically with this standard, judges may disqualify or penalize students for reading tablature or reading from music that has note names and fret placements written in. Once again, if the guidelines for note reading are not clear in your area, push for clarity.

Finally, as in all performances, students should dress for success. Ensemble students should wear the school concert attire or some form of matching outfits that indicate that the members of the ensemble are a team. Soloists should dress as if they were performing publicly. As a director, you should be aware of the attire expectations for a particular festival or competition and guide your students accordingly. The key takeaway here is that all students should dress as though this event were important even if there are no specific guidelines in order to make a good impression.

Creating Solo and Ensemble Opportunities

A solo and ensemble festival is usually an annual event for all areas of music education. If you are teaching mariachi, rock band, bluegrass, or other innovative ensembles, and your area offers solo and ensemble options to these students, chances are that this was not the case until someone stepped up and pushed to create an opportunity for these students. If your students are not being offered the same opportunities as band, choir, and orchestra, then as an innovative ensemble teacher, you are responsible for making their voices heard by the leadership of your state MEA. It is not likely that leadership of the MEA is going to reach out to guitar teachers proactively. Instead, teachers collectively need to be vocal if guitar or other students are being excluded.

Let's look at a case study. In 2000 in Nevada, students in band, choir, and orchestra in the Clark County School District had a scheduled, annual solo and ensemble day organized by the Nevada Music Educators Association (NMEA). At the time, there was nothing for guitar. One teacher was determined to have guitar students included in this event. Several months before this annual event, that teacher made numerous phone calls and wrote letters. The next thing you knew, an opportunity opened up for guitar students to register and participate. The words *inclusion* and *equal opportunity* did not have the weight then that they have today, but they were effective enough to convince state leaders to include guitar students in this event. The state MEA would not have reached out and included guitar without a little coaxing. This is another role of the teacher: to be a strong advocate for your innovative program. If you would like to see your students who belong to innovative ensembles have the same opportunities as band, choir, and orchestra students, it usually requires effort to make it happen. Sometimes, it takes a lot of effort.

This solo and ensemble festival was set up so that every student would receive a blue medal for Superior, a red medal for Excellent, and/or a red, white, and blue medal for Good. In most cases, students received either blue or red medals. This was a perfect outcome in the early years because guitar students needed the opportunity to attend an event, play in front of a judge, and receive a score and encouragement. Students receiving a blue medal during the first round could play again at the regional level. Those receiving a blue medal at the regional would then be considered for the state level.

It took four years before the NMEA felt the guitar students were good enough to compete at the state level, but it did happen. In 2004, the Las

Vegas Academy of the Arts had the first guitar quartet go to state and win Command Performance, which is the highest level for solo and ensemble in the state. This initial success has led to other successes, and a guitar soloist or a small guitar ensemble has won Command Performance every year since.

By 2004, so many guitar students participating in the first round of solo and ensemble, that the NMEA had to have four rooms to accommodate just the guitarists. To audition, each student paid a registration fee, which was to be used partially to pay for the judges, with money left over. Despite their initial lack of interest in including guitar students, the NMEA ended up making money. This is a real selling point if you want to start up participation in solo and ensemble events in your area.

While the annual NMEA solo and ensemble festival is still a wonderful opportunity, guitar students wanted more. Students were thrilled to receive a blue medal, but were eager to know of all of the blue medal winners, who was the best?

In 2011, teachers organized and started the first Best in Southern Nevada Guitar Solo and Ensemble Festival. During this two-round event, judges look for the top ten soloists, top three duos, top three trios, and top three quartets in the school district. Each year since 2011, the competition has started with approximately a hundred soloists. During the first round, half are eliminated, and the remaining contenders compete two weeks later for the top ten spots. Similarly, half the ensembles are eliminated during the first round of the competition and the ones that get through are rated for the first, second, and third spots in their categories. Teachers then host a Best in Southern Nevada Guitar Solo and Ensemble Winners' Recital featuring the winners. Each school represented receives a wall plaque for their accomplishments.

While this competition is open to every guitar student in high school, it is really geared for the most serious students who want something more than receiving a blue medal at the NMEA festival. Importantly, however, students are encouraged to participate in both events, which are scheduled so that there are no conflicts.

Both the NMEA solo and ensemble and the Best of Southern Nevada Guitar Solo and Ensemble festival are annual events that were originally created by a single music educator wanting opportunities for his students. If you teach in a school district or a state where these kinds of events are already in place for your innovative ensemble, it is your role as a teacher to prepare your students and encourage them to participate. In many cases, however, such events and opportunities may not already be in place for your innovative ensemble. If so, consider creating a structure like a solo and ensemble festival. Experience indicates that these events have proven to be real motivators because they give students a reason to become serious about performing at higher levels.

Starting a District Honor Guitar Ensemble

Imagine that your music program is a sporting team. What structures can be put into place to make your program function more like a sports team? School teams tend to compete with other schools in their district and region. The innovative programs should have the same opportunities, but at first without competition. Instead, new innovative programs should be able to perform for other school programs in the district and in the region.

If there is currently nothing in place in your district, be aware that someone must start the ball rolling. Be that person.

Here is a real model. Parts of this model may be applicable to your situation.

It was the year 2000 in the Clark County School District in Nevada. There were five middle schools and one high school with guitar programs. Guitar was thus being offered in the district for grade levels 6–12. Middle schools had levels 6, 7, and 8. High schools had levels 9–12. Assuming they attended a middle school with a guitar program, a student could take beginning guitar class in sixth grade and study guitar for seven years, but few ever did. The sixth graders who started in beginning guitar often stayed with guitar classes through middle school and quit once they had started high school. High school students often did not start beginning guitar until the later years when there were more elective hours to fill.

In theory, beginning guitar is the same if it is taught to a sixth grader or an eleventh grader. While the high school students are older, they also have more distractions and often do not practice as much as a middle school student. The bottom line is there was little difference in skill between an intermediate/advanced middle school class and an intermediate/advanced high school class.

Instead of seeing five middle schools and one high school, this school district looked at it as six schools having guitar classes with intermediate and advanced students. The six directors got together and selected six songs that were level appropriate for the time. Each director then selected the students who would take something like this repertoire seriously and learn the music for a collective performance. It was entitled Directors' Choice Honor Guitar Ensemble, and being selected was promoted as an honor. Because the ensemble music was arranged for three parts, each director selected multiples of three and assigned the parts to students. Each school could send a maximum of nine students.

It was agreed that one of the six schools would host this event and it would be held on a Saturday. The directors agreed on which Saturday and that was calendared and made public to all involved. A two-hour rehearsal led to a concert for the parents. The directors worked together during the rehearsal. It was a concentrated effort and a huge success for those students involved. Each student who participated received a printed certificate suitable for framing. The concert was video recorded, and many photos were taken for the purpose of promoting the next event the following year.

This has become an annual event in Clark County ever since. There have been many changes, of course. Many more schools were added to the district over the years and, as a result, the number of guitar classes also grew. In some years, each ensemble has numbered over a hundred participants, so what were previously small honor groups have become large ensembles. Students now pay a small fee, which pays for a commemorative T-shirt, a certificate, and pizza between the rehearsal and performance.

In 2008, the high school students began their own ensemble separate from the middle school students. Over the years, the high school ensemble has evolved into an audition requirement and is now known as the District Honor Guitar Ensemble. The school district pays to bring in a noted guitar educator as a special guest conductor and two days of rehearsals precede the performance. Students who are accepted into this ensemble are then eligible to audition for the all-state ensemble. Students who make the all-state ensemble may also audition for the NAfME All-National Honor Guitar Ensemble.

What did the guitar directors in the Clark County School District do right? First, by offering guitar students the same opportunities as students enrolled in band, choir, and orchestra, they made these students feel that they are as important as or equal to other music students in their individual schools. Second, the guitar directors elevated guitar education not only within the school district, but also on a national scale, because they created an opportunity to hire out-of-district guests to conduct the honor ensembles and the All-State ensemble. Nationally recognized guitar educators now desire an invitation to conduct one of these two honor ensembles each year. This was a big step in putting the Clark County School District on the national map for guitar education. The guitar directors involved worked together with the focus of doing what was good for students without egos getting in the way and without feelings of competitiveness. These efforts represent collaboration at its best.

School District Festivals

Many school districts have ensemble festivals for band, choir, and orchestra. In states that have a good deal of guitar education in schools, there are also ensemble festivals for guitar ensemble. If there is not one in your area, consider creating one.

For educators in an area where guitar ensemble festivals are an annual event, your intermediate and/or advanced guitar ensembles are expected to participate. Generally, the model for this type of event is to have multiple judges who score the ensemble's performance and give one of four scores: Superior, Excellent, Good, and Fair. Superior is the rating everyone wants to leave with, because this is the highest score possible. Generally, school districts will provide a plaque with the name of the school, the school year, the director's name, and an indication that the rating is Superior. They sometimes also do so for the next best rating, which is Excellent. The third score is, of course, Good, which no one really wants to receive, and the last score, Fair, is rarely ever given, because it does not help students in any way. If an ensemble is that unprepared, they already know it.

The nice thing about this scoring system is that there is no limit to how many ensembles can receive the top score. In other words, this is not a competition. It is an opportunity to hear other schools perform and receive feedback from quality adjudicators. To be an award-winning guitar program, the ensemble of course sets its goal to receive a Superior or Excellent.

Not all schools do so, but some schools consider the score of the ensemble at district festival as a part of the director's annual teacher evaluation. Administrators will often read and consider the previous year's evaluation before writing the current evaluation, and the same might be true in considering district festival scores. If the teacher received a Superior rating the previous year and another one the current year, then the administrator might take this honor as a sign that the teacher is an effective educator. The same can hold true in the event that the guitar ensemble receives two consecutive

Good or Fair ratings. An administrator will be more apt to look more deeply at other aspects of the teacher and may become suspicious of the director's skills as an educator.

Before arriving at the festival, the festival organizer will most likely have had multiple contacts and provided such details with each of the participants as the schedule, what is expected, what type of music to select, who is judging, and what judges will be listening for. This way, ensemble directors can help their students prepare for the event and have a clear idea what will be included in the adjudication.

Though it should be made clear what elements are used to create a score, be aware that other elements are not scored but often observed. Here are some thoughts to consider when you are preparing for a guitar ensemble festival.

While this factor has never been a part of the festival evaluation, watching what happens once a bus has arrived at a festival and observing how a school guitar ensemble gets off the bus and congregates can be very revealing. Some ensembles depart the bus in a straight line—with the students dressed for the stage, carrying everything they need to perform—in a quiet and orderly fashion. If the director needs to give directions, they may do so without having to try to get the attention of the group. Though this behavior has nothing to do with how well the ensemble performs together, it is impressive to see; observers may be more interested in hearing this group perform because they expect the group's organization and maturity also to be reflected in their performance.

In contrasts, imagine that another bus arrives and the students jump off in a rowdy and chaotic manner. Some have left items that they must go back and retrieve. The director is screaming out orders, and the students do not appear to be listening. Instead, students are congregated in small groups and are not dressed for the stage. Though this behavior has nothing to do with how well this ensemble performs together, it can make a negative first impression.

Buses arrive throughout the day and ensembles deboard buses in a variety of ways. Though this behavior is not part of the evaluation, know that someone is observing and possibly forming an impression of your group.

Similarly, dressing appropriately is important for making a good impression—for both students and teachers. Some teachers might come dressed in formal wear such as a full tuxedo or concert dress. Others come in nice suits or blazers with dress shirt and tie, or a dress or tailored outfit.

Others wear jeans and a T-shirt or a polo-style shirt. Whatever it means to you, dress for success. Though "how the director dresses" is not a part of the score sheet, it certainly will have an effect on the adjudicators.[1]

The members of the ensemble should also dress for success. Again, this factor may not be a part of the evaluation leading to the final score but *looking* like an award-winning ensemble can often help you *become* an award-winning ensemble. Some ensembles wear tuxedos, other wear suits, some wear the traditional white dress shirt and black pants or skirt, and some wear matching T-shirts. Recently concert wear has been criticized by some educators as elitist or gender-restrictive. The point here is not to mandate a specific dress code, but to highlight that how your ensemble dresses *is* important in making a good impression. Find the appropriate dress code that feels right for your specific ensemble and students, and for your specific performance situation. It does not necessarily need to be formal, but it should represent a collaborative effort of teamwork.

Once the ensemble has stepped off the bus at the time of arrival, how do students walk into the building? Are they walking in a straight line? Do they chatter while they are walking in? Are students banging their guitar cases against the doorframe when they are entering the building? Does the ensemble give the sense that the members know which direction to go once they are inside the building? Similarly, how do students walk into the warm-up room? How organized is the group? What do students do with their cases? How quickly can students get into place and begin the warm-up session? Is the director in control? Do they have a tuning procedure that makes sense in terms of how little time there is in the warm-up room? Does the ensemble have a warm-up procedure or go straight to ensemble playing? These are all factors that should be discussed, planned, and practiced prior to arrival at a guitar ensemble festival.

Once the warm-up time is over, in most cases the ensemble will need to move to the performance space. Are there clear instructions about how the ensemble is going to transfer to the performance space in terms of what to do with such items as music, instruments, cases, footstools, and tuners? How well does the ensemble clean up and put things back in place when leaving the warm-up room?

Lining up to enter the stage is usually the first time the ensemble comes in the sight of the adjudicators. Are the students being quiet? Do they have their instruments, music, footstools, tuners, or anything else they may need to perform? As students take the stage, is there logic in the manner in which students sit? Are students sitting so that all of the same parts are sitting together? Are part-one students on the left side, on the right side, or in the middle? The adjudicators may consider these factors. The placement will not be as important unless the balance of the ensemble is not good. Then placement will play a part in the overall score.

Once students are on stage, the evaluation and score keeping begin. Most festivals have guidelines that every ensemble will need to follow. For example, the conductor will need to provide original copies of the music for each of the judges. The festival organizer will provide information regarding how many judges will be involved, which scales will need to be performed, if sight-reading will be required, and any other pertinent details that will affect the judging.

Some festivals have an evaluation period prior to performing during which a judge may check to see that all students are playing from modern staff notation and no tablature or note names are written on the music. Music may also be checked for copyright to make sure that copyright laws are being followed. This is an important consideration when ensembles are performing free music retrieved and printed from the Internet, because most free Internet music is copyrighted. Printing and performing this music even though it is freely available online may violate copyright laws. Some festivals do not allow ensembles to perform Internet music without a letter of permission from the publisher. If you purchase music online, you should have a copy of the receipt and a publisher's letter giving permission to perform the music at a festival. Many publishers provide this documentation with each purchase.

Some festivals provide a common piece in which every ensemble will perform. Doing so makes judging a little easier so that every ensemble can be compared to one another on at least one piece. In most cases, ensemble festivals would like to hear three pieces of contrasting styles. If one piece is a common piece, then the director has the option of choosing two additional titles. Judges will consider if the three pieces are contrasting in style, tempo, and time signature. Generally speaking, for a guitar ensemble festival it is considered a plus if the director chooses one piece by a composer who is currently living. This option does not mean the piece needs to be a pop tune, but contemporary in terms of composition within the current decade. The conductor will provide scores to each of the judges so they will be able to make an assessment of the repertoire selected.

Even though the ensemble may not have yet played the first note, the judges will make assessments about what types of guitars the ensemble is using. Are the students playing all of the same types of guitars, either all nylon string or all steel string? Is there a mix of the two? Is the ensemble extending the range of the guitar by added contra basses or electric bass on the low end and/or octave guitars on the high end?

The judges will also make an assessment about how the students are holding the instruments. Are the students using some form of "rest position," meaning holding the instrument so it is not making any sound? When students move to playing position, are they all using the same sitting position? Posture will most likely be a part of the evaluation that will count towards the final score. Are all students using picks? Are all students playing finger style? Is there a mix of pick users and finger-style players within the ensemble? If so, this combination may count toward the final score.

As the ensemble begins to perform the first selection, the judges will take notice if the director is conducting or just marking time through hand jesters. Is the conductor using a baton? Is the director conducting dynamics, phrasing, and musical expressions, or just keeping time? Is the ensemble changing dynamics, timbre, and/or tempo in order to be more expressive and demonstrate overall musicianship? Are the students looking at the director? Are the students following the director's gestures?

As the ensemble continues its program, judges will consider if the selections of music are well within the range of skill of the ensemble. Are the pieces too hard or too easy? Are there sections of the pieces that the ensemble is struggling to perform correctly? Picking music that is too hard or too easy can affect the overall scoring.

Finally, once an ensemble's performance is complete, the judges will indicate that it is time to clear the stage and the ensemble will leave. Be mindful that the ensemble is in view of the judges and anyone in the audience. Are the students clear about how they are going to exit the stage? Are they walking in a straight line? Do they have their instruments, music, footstools, tuners, and any other equipment that was needed for their performance?

All this may seem like a great deal to consider when students and teachers are attending a guitar ensemble festival, but it is good to know how everything is going to work from the time the bus arrives until the time the bus departs. Students should also be made aware of behavioral expectations as well as appearance and attire.

Preparing for an ensemble festival is more than just practicing the same three pieces over and over. Students should be provided with direction about what will happen once the group has arrived and what is expected while they are attending the festival. Ultimately, any mishaps while at the festival reflect on the director. Prepare to be an award-wining ensemble from the moment of arrival.

8

Travel and Off-Campus Performances

In college, music education majors are prepared for teaching jobs in a variety of ways, but the topic of traveling with future students rarely comes up. In fact, it is possible that this topic is never discussed in a university setting, even though traveling is usually an important part of a music teacher's job description. I've met music educators who have been teaching for many years, and it is amazing to hear about all of the places they have traveled to with their school music ensembles—ranging from local trips to foreign countries.

I've heard stories of students traveling to New York City to perform at Carnegie Hall or in the Macy's Thanksgiving Day Parade; marching in the Rose Bowl Parade in Pasadena, California; playing in cathedrals in Italy, and on and on. This is not to mention all of the trips to Disneyland, Disneyworld, Six Flags, Knotts Berry Farm, SeaWorld, and Universal Studios.

These stories make the job sound like a whole lot of fun, especially because in many cases, the director is not required to pay to attend these trips. So, each year does the director get to take the students on a trip and go for free? Who wouldn't want to travel to these places? Yet traveling with children who are not your own is a great deal of responsibility; the catalog of what can go wrong is endless. Traveling can be a high-pressure situation, and it is likely that there will be little or no rest until the group returns home safe and sound. All this is why well-organized trips will often include parent chaperones and school administrators to help shoulder some of the responsibilities.

Traveling with the right group of students and chaperones is key to a successful trip. Travel is also not cheap, and students will need to take some financial responsibility for paying their part of the trip, often by participating in school-organized fundraisers. Planning travel, then, requires of an ensemble director a significant time commitment and the organizational savvy to coordinate between many different groups. This chapter makes the case for why travel is important, how to optimize travel and performance opportunities for your students, and how to navigate the complexities that come with these off-campus performance events.

Building an Award-Winning Guitar Program. Bill Swick, Oxford University Press. © Oxford University Press 2022.
DOI: 10.1093/oso/9780197609804.003.0008

Why Travel?

Traveling with students is a big responsibility, is costly, and requires good organization. In spite of the most careful planning, however, much can go wrong. So why travel? One simple answer is that travel can create lifelong memories. Decades after leaving school, music students can still vividly recollect school trips, and these memories are often some of the first that a student will recall when thinking about their time in school. Blending music educational or performance experiences with travel can make a significant long-term impact on the lives of your students—whether or not they pursue music in their lives in the future. In addition, some students have not experienced being on an eight-hour bus ride, or have never flown on an airplane or shared a hotel room with anyone other than family members. School travel has a way of presenting many "firsts" for students. In my case, most of our travel is the first time students visit a university campus, attend master classes, perform on an acoustically perfect stage, and hear recitals by world-class performers. These experiences can have a long-term, positive effect.

Another simple yet especially important answer is that travel results in bonding. During trips, students have experiences with other students that bring them closer. This greater sense of community will manifest in the quality of your ensemble when the group returns and starts playing music together at school. Ensembles are about working together to create music, and the performance will be improved if the relationships among those in the ensemble have also improved.

One outstanding music director, Rick McEnaney, so believes in the importance of bonding through travel that he will organize a trip to nowhere at the beginning of each school year just to get the music students out of the classroom and on a bus together. McEnaney's students will drive for two hours in one direction, stop, have lunch, and drive back. This trip may seem an odd use of time and resources, but the students love it, and it pays off in that the ensemble gets along much better. By bonding early on, the students are more likely to work well with one another. In addition, these bonds among the students create a sense of community and a feeling of belonging, which also motivate them to perform: the music is better because students want to impress one another, and not let down their team.

Among many good reasons for travel, these two—creating lifelong memories and opportunities for your ensemble to bond—are significant enough to justify scheduling at least one trip a year. Some programs will schedule a trip each semester. The earlier in the school year you can arrange the trip or trips, the better.

If you are teaching in an environment that is economically challenged, you may be reading this chapter and thinking that travel is out of the question. To say travel is expensive is an understatement. Everything about travel costs money. If your program or students have no means of funding, it is easy just to forget about travel. And yet educators like Jim Yancey (who taught in the most economically challenged area in Arizona) have made it happen for their programs despite financial difficulties. Yancey is well known for taking his students on major trips, frequently to foreign countries. How did he do it? First, he had a strong vision. He imagined traveling with his students and taking them to places they might otherwise not get to see and experience during their school years. Yancey envisioned the music program as a means to expose students to new parts of the world, and in exchange, these students would impress audiences everywhere they went with their musical talents.[1] Yancey convinced his high school students that they could play as well as anyone their age living anywhere—something that every good educator should do. He encouraged them to work hard and to put everything into learning, practicing, and performing beautiful music together. Meanwhile, he spent much of his free time in writing grants, contacting businesses, and creating promotions on social media to raise money for travel. The story is inspiring, but it is also more than that. It is a model, showing that it can be done. Anyone who shares the vision can make it a reality. Let John Maxwell remind you, "Teamwork makes the dream work."[2]

Many other models might inspire you or your program. One music educator in Minneapolis, Minnesota, does more than a simple trip every year. Ruth LeMay's program takes an annual ten-day tour across multiple states. In her model, only the older students are included in the annual tour and get the benefits of experiencing this major trip firsthand. Yet, as LeMay explains, the younger students who are not going on the trip get to observe the preparation for the tour during the months and weeks leading up to departure and hear the stories and laughter upon the older students' return. A result is that the younger students are hooked on the idea and totally focused on working to be prepared so that they will qualify for the tour when they are old enough. LeMay adds that the annual tour has become one of the main highlights of her program.[3]

In general, LeMay promotes traveling as much as possible with as many students as possible. Traveling, she suggests, does not always need to be as extravagant as a ten-day tour; it can be as simple as a taking the city bus for an afternoon performance at a local business. She agrees that travel promotes lifelong memories, creates friendships, and is an important bonding experience for the ensemble.

Education versus Vacation

Including students in decision-making when it comes to travel leads to ownership and responsibility. Yet it is important to balance student interests with your educational goals. When students are asked where they would like to go if they could take a trip, the answers tend to be all over the place, but will almost never be "let's go to a college campus and sit through a classical guitar recital." Instead, the most common responses will be amusement parks or exotic vacation locations.

Your role as the ensemble director is to tie travel to educational experiences. Some might say that all travel is an educational experience, and perhaps that is correct. If your goal is to build an award-winning music program, however, you should be more strategic in your travel. For instance, there may be an opportunity to perform or compete in a festival that is a state or two away. Though group bonding is a major reason to travel, as highlighted earlier, traveling to perform or compete will do more for your program in an educational sense than a trip to an amusement park. In addition, students might bring home a certificate or plaque or another piece of hardware that they can proudly display on the walls, indicating to others that the group has traveled and has been recognized for an outstanding performance.

After returning, make it a point to share photos with the administrator who is in charge of activities along with a short story of what the students did, the details of the festival, and any recognition the ensemble may have received. Share the information with the school principal. Do not be shy about letting people know that your ensemble traveled to perform in an out-of-district festival. These are important steps toward building an award-winning program.

Why College Campuses?

Some of the award-winning guitar programs at the university level have learned that hosting an annual festival is a great way to recruit new students.

It is also a way to receive national recognition and, in some cases, international recognition. The school-of-music programs that understand *the importance* of attracting pre-college students to their campuses tend then to also *actually* attract the young talent needed to keep their programs vibrant.

Music festivals frequently offer opportunities for pre-college ensembles to perform and participate in master classes, lectures, and recitals given by high-caliber performers. Universities often schedule high-profile artists and, in some cases, international artists to perform at their annual music festivals. In addition, the program's faculty is available to meet with prospective students and talk about the offerings of their program.

Taking students to one of these festivals is in many respects a home run. High school students are given the freedom to explore a university campus, perform in a world-class performance hall, learn through lectures and master classes, and attend performances by world-class artists. This type of travel has many benefits. Often the information students are exposed to while attending a college music festival starts showing up in the classroom a week or two later. The habits that I have witnessed most commonly are students shaping their fingernails and focusing on tone production, using professional-quality strings, focusing on posture, and playing newly purchased music while at a festival. Students may have been exposed to these elements in the classroom, witnessing these practices modeled by a world-class guitarist makes them real.

Setting Travel Goals

In the early years of any new program, the idea of travel may seem farfetched or simply out of reach. One of the ways to make travel a reality is to set realistic short-term goals that are achievable in the first few years, as well as longer-term goals. Each of your goals should have a defined timeline. Including travel as a tangible annual goal is one way to keep track of whether you are meeting the targets you have set for your program while also benefiting from the experience that only travel can bring.

While setting long-term travel goals, make sure to include one that will represent the absolute pinnacle of achievement for your program. For example, a popular goal for many music educators is to perform in Carnegie Hall. If you make that your goal, you will know that you have an award-winning program (as you define it) on the date that you perform in Carnegie

Hall. These big goals are important to have—goals that may be daunting but still realistic and obtainable.

In addition to these large long-term goals, set annual goals that will happen in a given school year. Take advantage of opportunities to perform each year at major music education conventions. To do so, you must usually pursue an application process that must be completed a year in advance. Many music educators set goals to perform at their MEA state conference. In addition, they may also apply for the Mid-West Conference in Chicago or the National Association for Music Education national conference. Innovative ensembles also frequently have a place to perform at the NAMM National Association of Music Merchants summer and winter international conventions. ASTA is yet another organization that has been open to some of the innovative ensembles and hosts an annual conference. Performing at these events is a big accomplishment and should be on your radar for building an award-winning music program.

Local Off-Campus Performances

Off-campus performances, even local ones, have the potential of becoming complicated. Before accepting any opportunities to perform off campus, make sure you understand all of the procedures related to students leaving campus. Check with the administrator assigned to school activities. This administrator will have all of the answers and will know what paperwork must be completed and all other details associated with travel. Seeing the word "travel" here might be confusing. Any time students leave the campus during the school day, even if it is just a block away, the process falls under the category of travel.

The school may have rules prohibiting students from leaving campus during the school day. If that is the case, then accepting performance opportunities during school hours may be out of the question, because leaving school during school hours simply may not be negotiable.

It is common for local professional organizations to contact a school to request entertainment for breakfast or lunch meetings. If your school allows you to participate in these types of community events, by all means go for it. If your school does not allow students to leave school during school hours, then you have no choice but to turn down these requests.

Schools also have guidelines about student performances off campus after school hours and on weekends. Any event requesting a performance scheduled after school, at night, or on a weekend will still require approval and paperwork. If students are representing the school while they are performing, they must have all of the paperwork completed and the administration needs to be aware that students are participating in an off-campus event. The details of transportation, expenses, who is chaperoning, the times students are leaving and returning, if school instruments will be used—all of these details must be documented prior to the event. Do not make the mistake of thinking because the event is after school that students can represent the school without paperwork and supervision.

Community Involvement

It is common to hear secondary school administrators talk about how schools need to be community minded, active, and involved. You would assume that schools encourage music ensembles to be active in community events and should be visible in demonstrating community involvement. Your students can be involved with community activities in many ways. Public libraries frequently provide opportunities for music ensembles to perform. Annual arts and crafts shows may support student entertainment. The Parks and Recreation Department may have opportunities for student performances. And don't forget senior homes, rehabilitation centers, and hospices looking for student talent to perform for special events. The holidays in particular often provide community opportunities for students to perform.

If you have an administrative team that supports community involvement, then have a conversation and ask the hard questions. Most school districts have clear guidelines regarding transportation. Some school districts allow students to drive themselves to a performance venue. Others do not. Do not guess; know for certain what the guidelines are and follow them. If your school does not allow students to drive themselves, then what services are available for transportation and who will pay the costs?

Some school districts have a strict requirement that a licensed schoolteacher be present for the entire time while students are off campus and performing at an event. If this is true for your school, does the licensed schoolteacher need to be you? If so, can you be paid for your time outside of school contract hours? Who will pay the cost? If you are not available, who will pay the cost for a different licensed schoolteacher to be present?

Some school districts require that the risk management office be notified in writing weeks before an off-campus event occurs. The risk management office calculates the risk of injury to students and provides insurance for each child in the event that an accident results in injury. Who will pay the risk management office for the insurance?

On the basis of these questions, it must be clear by now that performing in the community for free can be costly. Chances are that the school will not be able to afford performing off campus for free on too many occasions. It depends on the rules of the school district, how closely they are followed, and how important it is to the school to appear community minded and for students to be seen performing in public places. As a general rule, do not commit to an off-campus performance without knowing all of the costs, what the responsibilities are, and how the costs will be covered.

Accepting Donations for Performances

Some school districts are set up to accept donations in exchange for student performances. Before booking any engagements, visit with the administrator in charge of activities as well as the school banker and have a clear understanding what is involved before accepting money for an engagement.

From time to time an organization or business will host an event in a hotel or reception hall and would like to add music. One of the organizers may know of your school or have a student in your program and contact you to perform for their event. In exchange for the student performance, the organization will make a cash contribution to your music program. That sounds reasonable. The donation may be large enough to cover any costs like transportation, insurance, and a licensed teacher, with money left over that will go directly into the music program.

This kind of event makes your program appear to be community minded. After all, your students are performing in public for a special event in the community. The organization is willing to make a donation that not only covers the costs of performing but also is a cash gift to your music program. In many aspects, this is a win/win. What could possibly be wrong with this scenario?

Possibly nothing. It could very well be a perfect scenario. It depends on where you live. If you live in an area where there are a lot of working, professional musicians, the music union representatives may see your school as a threat for taking away possible employment from working musicians. This reaction is particularly true if students are performing in a hotel ballroom, a convention center, a reception hall, a wedding chapel, or any other venue that would typically hire professional musicians for the same event. This is information worth learning about before accepting an engagement. Consulting with the activities administrator prior to agreeing to perform is always a good idea. If there is a musicians' union hall in your community, it may be worthwhile getting to know the secretary and asking questions to avoid hard feelings or even litigation.

If you find that accepting donations for performances works well, then by all means do as many as you can. Document all performances, even the ones you perform for free, to confirm how actively you are performing in the community. No performance is too small to be documented. Keep good records of performances and share your activities with your administration and parents. This information can also be used to complete the schoolwide community service hours report that is done once a year.

9

Funding Your Program

Why do students share instruments and not each have their own? Why do the guitar strings on a particular instrument appear as if they had never been changed? Why are students playing music found free on the Internet? Why are there no footstools? And the questions go on and on. Often the answer is the same for all of these and other related questions: *funding*.

All music programs require money that comes either directly from the school or through fundraisers. This chapter walks you through the complexities of funding in a school setting, underlines the importance of advocating for funding where it exists, and offers ideas and practical tips for fundraisers and other financial alternatives.

Asking for Funding

One of the most frustrating words to hear from other music educators is that their students do not have everything they need for the teacher to properly teach the class, much less build a program. These directors will say that they have asked their principal or administrative supervisor for money for such necessities as method books, music, strings, and instruments, and the answer has always been "no."

Yes, perhaps a request was made that was denied—it does happen—yet often the denial is not the whole picture. Was the director told there is no money *this minute* to fund a class? In some cases, the director may have asked one time, was told "no," and then never asked again, assuming that just because there was no money to fund classes at that moment, there never would be. As a result, the students in their program miss out.

Money is a complicated subject when it comes to schools. School districts have an assortment of "pots" of money, meaning that some money may be spent only for teachers' salaries, and others only for textbooks. Money may be just for uniforms, or for paper and supplies. The list goes on and on. A school may have a lot of money, but that money is earmarked for items that do not

Building an Award-Winning Guitar Program. Bill Swick, Oxford University Press. © Oxford University Press 2022.
DOI: 10.1093/oso/9780197609804.003.0009

assist the music teacher. Even though a guitar teacher might have asked for money that was sitting in a now depleted pot, however, maybe there is a different pot full of money that could be of help. For example, perhaps there is no money for ensemble arrangements, but plenty of money for textbooks. For guitar class, music *is* the textbook. Can method books and ensemble arrangements thus be paid for by the money earmarked for textbooks rather than money that might have been earmarked for elective classes?

Each school district receives a fixed amount of money per student. This amount of money varies from state to state and district to district. Students attending schools in small towns may bring more money per student than students in large cities. Schools in low-income areas may receive more money per student than schools in wealthier areas. It is complicated. The bulk of the money per student is going toward teachers' salaries. Beyond that expense is a laundry list of items that must be funded. When all is said and done, a small percentage is in theory divided into the seven or eight classes each student attends. In other words, depending on the total class size, each student has some cash value to your classroom.

Does guitar class then get the same amount of money as band? That depends. If band has seventy students and guitar has twenty students, band in theory will receive three and a half times more money than guitar. With only twenty students, there may not be enough money for new instruments, but there should be money to purchase supplies like strings, picks, footstools, and music. Are there ways you can be creative and refer to these things by different names to qualify for funding from pots that have more money?

Be the squeaky wheel that gets the grease. Remember that the teachers who ask the most receive the most, whereas the teachers who never ask rarely receive anything extra. Some teachers choose to remain quiet, believing that what is needed to teach students will be provided, and if not, they will just manage to get by—or worse, reach into their own pockets and purchase necessary items. Before going without the materials, ask for assistance and then ask again. Keep asking until your students have what they need for you to be an effective teacher and for students to become effective learners.

What if Someone Else Asks?

This next suggestion is tricky. Though it does not seem right, sometimes when a parent from the program's parent organization asks for financial support, a principal may find a way to provide what was denied to the teacher, particularly if the parent asks during a public forum. The downside is that the principal may feel pressured to provide financial assistance and possibly publicly humiliated and then hold it against the teacher. If parents feel the need to ask for financial support, it needs to be their idea.

It is so important to have a parent organization and have parents who are willing to attend meetings with the principal and stand up for the guitar program. For example, if a guitar parent makes an observation during a parent meeting that the band students just received new uniforms and new instruments, and are going on a trip requiring air travel, then the guitar parent may ask, "Why do the guitar students play on old instruments and old strings and have no money for music?" Keep in mind this parent is standing up for their child and the other students in these classes.

The principal may reply that this year is the year for band and elective funding was spent on getting the band up to speed because they are marching in the Rose Bowl Parade or something just as significant. The principal may go on to say that next year will be orchestra's year because they will be performing at the Midwest Conference or something along those lines. That response sounds logical. It makes perfect sense. And what the principal is also saying is that these two programs are award-winning departments that have each accomplished some form of national recognition and each must have what it needs to represent the school, the school district, and the state. Perhaps at this moment the need to showcase that your guitar program is also an award-winning program, or on its way there, becomes clear. Where is the guitar ensemble traveling in order to represent the school?

Student Class Fees

School districts have various ways of handling school class fees. Once there was a time when classes that required the use of disposable materials were allowed to charge fees, particularly if they were electives. For an art class, for example, that requires paints and special paper, or a ceramics class that uses clay and plaster, these materials need to be replenished regularly and require funding. For guitar class, strings need to be replaced regularly, an expense that is otherwise not funded. One solution is to collect a class fee from students.

Some schools allow such a fee to be collected at the beginning of the year. It then becomes the responsibility of the teacher to document how the money collected is spent on students' supplies. In some cases, the class fee covers the cost of the required method book, solo and ensemble music, supplementary instruction materials, and possibly a required shirt used as a performance uniform. All of these items are used and kept by the students. Teachers are required to maintain accurate documentation of how class-fee money is spent as well as a justification for the need for these materials. If you are able to collect a fee for your classes, the details of the amount, how it should be paid, and when it is due should be included in your class handbook and on your dedicated website. Along with describing the fees, you should list the materials that students will receive in exchange for the class fee.

Some schools charge forty dollars per elective class. If there are a hundred students enrolled in the total number of elective classes taught by the same teacher, the teacher will receive $4,000 to cover the costs of materials needed for all of the elective classes. From this money, the teacher will provide students with instructional materials otherwise not funded by the school. In addition, the teacher will be able to cover some of the expenses associated with making sure that all instruments are playable and in good working order—including guitar strings.

If class fees are permissible in your school, this is a way to fund the daily expenses, funding that is in many cases a big relief. Without this money, there may be students going without instructional materials, and the cost of instrument maintenance may sideline instruments from being used until money is available to repair them.

Financial Alternatives

Let us go back to the scenario in which a teacher asked the school principal for financial assistance and was denied. At that moment, the teacher should also ask if there are any financial alternatives to receiving funding. Before agreeing to sell candy bars, candles, and/or magazine subscriptions, first ask if it is permissible to charge an admission to guitar performances at school. Some schools allow it; others do not. If there is no funding for guitar classes, perhaps the guitar performance could be an exception. Continue by asking if it is possible to accept money for off-campus performances by the guitar students. This is another issue that varies from school to school. Ask if it is permissible to accept cash donations from parents and patrons.

It is possible to fully fund a guitar program with monies from ticket sales to performances, community performances, and donations. Guitar teachers should never have to start drives to sell magazine subscriptions, catalog items, candy, or coupon books. It is a big plus to advertise that guitar students will never be asked to sell anything. Some parents will gladly make a cash donation in exchange for not having to participate in fundraising.

If it is permissible to sell tickets to school performances, consider bundling the whole year into one price. The number of performances will be known, and the dates should be set on the calendar. Decide on the price of admission tickets, add it up, and sell a season ticket that is good for all performances. This way you can capture a year's worth of admission tickets all at once at the beginning of the year so that you will have money for such necessities as music, instruments, and strings. Price this season ticket at less than the cost of purchasing each ticket separately. Make it available for sale the first month of school, with the goal of collecting enough money to start the new school year strong. You should then be able to purchase the materials and equipment needed to be an effective educator.

Fundraising Ideas

As a music educator in a public school, you have a good chance of finding many opportunities for fundraisers. Or the opportunities will find you, and those who manage fundraising programs will seek you out. These promotions often sound like a good idea at first. Selling chocolate bars for one dollar is easy and students start out with enthusiasm—what could go wrong? Then there's that one student who sells a box of candy bars and then accidently loses the money collected. What do you do then? What happens the day after the candy is delivered and it becomes apparent that ants have discovered the candy before sales begin? What happens when other insects infiltrate the inventory? Who pays for the chocolate bars?

Fundraisers by nature take up more time than you might guess, and much can go wrong. The amount of money earned is sometimes not worth the effort, not to mention the strain that fundraising can put on parents. Parents who have participated in student fundraisers frequently say they would rather make a cash donation just to avoid being part of fundraising. Yet sometimes fundraising cannot be avoided and can be an important source of revenue for some programs. Following are some ideas for fundraising.

Holiday Pie Sale

If you live in a metropolitan area, chances are there will be a wholesale bakery in the area. If there is a wholesale bakery that specializes in pies, having a pie sale for the holidays is a great fundraising opportunity. To make the choices easy, select a limited number of flavors, such as pumpkin, pecan, apple, chocolate, lemon, and coconut. Add five dollars to the wholesale price of each pie and take orders shortly after the school year begins with a clear date for when the pies will be delivered—typically, the last school day before Thanksgiving and the last school day before winter break. Work with the school banker to set up online orders and make it clear that each purchase is a donation to your program and therefore tax deductible.

One high school music program has an annual sale and sells a thousand pies every year. If pies are left over, they easily freeze and can be sold frozen. The money comes early in the school year and takes care of much of the funding needs of the program. Depending on your location, if pies are not available, consider other options that may be popular for the holidays.

Annual Faculty Talent Show

Consider hosting an annual faculty talent show. This is a collaborative effort that has been successful in a number of schools. Advertise your show early in the year as an annual "fun raiser." Find faculty members who have real talent and work with them to provide some quality entertainment. Then encourage other faculty members to lip-sync or dance or do anything that will get them on stage and seen by the audience.

Students love seeing the faculty perform both seriously and just for fun. This show can become an annual event. Each year, the audience will get bigger because the word will get out about how much fun it is to attend. These shows need to be priced to be affordable, but high enough that they are clearly fundraisers. Each year, you should inform the attendees how the money is going to be used. One year, the money might purchase uniforms for the mariachi ensemble. Another year the money might purchase new guitars for the guitar program. Everyone participating should be aware that this is a collaborative effort to do some good for a school or program for which there is currently no funding.

Pie in the Face

This idea may in some way be combined with an annual faculty talent show. While you are not likely to raise a lot of money with this fundraiser, if you need only a hundred dollars, and need it quickly, this plan may work. Ask faculty members to volunteer to allow students to hit them in the face with a cream pie. Get some large garbage bags from the janitorial staff for teachers to wear over their clothes and set up a station outdoors during lunchtime. For only five dollars, students may purchase a pie tin filled with whipped cream and put it in the face of one of the participating teachers. If possible, convince an administrator or two to volunteer as well. Make sure to have someone taking plenty of photos and have an abundance of tins and whipped cream. Once this event gets started, you may be surprised how many students can find five dollars and are willing to participate.

Online Sales

There is simply no better way to raise money than through passive income—in other words, through minimal effort. Amazon offers a program for schools called AmazonSmile that pays schools 0.5 percent of online sales that are directed to Amazon from a school website. This program is rather easy to join but it does take some effort to remind students and parents to use this feature when they are purchasing from Amazon.

Amazon also has the Amazon Associate Program, which pays much better. Schools receive up to 10 percent of sales, depending on the products. There is an application process, and it does require more time to manage. Records provided by Amazon indicate that some schools have made tens of thousands of dollars by being a part of this program. This fundraising would require a parent volunteer or someone who has the time to manage the program, but it could turn out to be very lucrative. The best part about this is students are not actively selling anything and are not handling money, and you are not juggling money and products. It is certainly worth looking into.

If you live in an area where there is a Krispy Kreme Doughnuts franchise, you may be able to participate in one of their online fundraising programs for schools. During the COVID-19 pandemic, Krispy Kreme has come up with a virtual contactless program that helps schools promote the sale of doughnuts. This sale is another way to passively make money without students being actively involved.

Online fundraising is a creative field and constantly changing. Do a simple Google search for online school fundraising and see what comes up. It may be worth your time.

Grants

Another possible solution is grants, which are typically funds given by some entity (i.e., a charitable foundation) for a specific purpose and are not expected to be returned or paid back. Years ago, the process for applying for a grant was tedious and required someone with experience in grant writing. Since then, grant applications have become much easier and much more available. You can find a listing of grants by doing a simple Google search for "music grants." That search alone will provide a significant list. Not all grants will apply to your situation, and you may have to look at the details of a large number of grants before finding one that suits your needs with an application that your program can fulfill.

Here is a list of ten music grants selected by Zach VanderGraaff from solfeg.io.[1] If you are interested in applying for one of these grants, take the time to look into the details of each one to see if it is a good fit for your program.

- American Country Music Lifting Lives Grant
- Kinder Morgan Grant
- National Endowment for the Arts
- Sharon Gewirtz Kids to Concerts
- Associated Chamber Music Players Grant
- BMI Foundation Grant
- Fender Music Foundation
- Mockingbird Foundation
- D'Addario Foundation
- ASCAP Foundation Grants

Be aware that many more music grants are available. The preceding are just a sampling of the grants that may be able to assist you in purchasing new instruments, strings, printed music, and/or other accessories. Some of these foundations provide only products and do not award cash. Take inventory and have clarity what your program really needs. You may not need cash as badly as you need new instruments or strings.

Donations

During the COVID-19 pandemic in 2020, many music educators realized their schools did not own enough instruments for every student who needed one to take home. It is one thing to have a complete classroom set of instruments that students share daily. It is quite another to provide instruments to every individual student. In the early months of the pandemic, there was a push to find instruments for students because so many schools had switched to long-distance learning.

If your program needs instruments or supplies, put that information on your website with details about how people can donate. If you have a parent organization, ask parents to make it a priority to acquire what your program needs. There are also organizations that help schools and students who need instruments. See, for example, Guitars for Kids at www.songbirdsfoundation. org, One Child. One Guitar. One Miracle. at Guitars not Guns at www. guitarsnotguns.org, Hungry for Music—Creating Smile . . . One Instrument at a Time. at www.hungryformusic.org, and others.

Though you might not live in a state where these organizations exist, you may find elements of each organization to copy in order to put your own program together. Do not be shy about letting others know what is needed to make certain that students are receiving what they need to learn.

It is amazing how many families have musical instruments sitting on a shelf, in a closet, or under a bed, and are more than happy to give them to a school. Pick a Saturday and have an instrument drop-off day when donors can drive to your school and bring musical instruments they are no longer using. My experience with this drive is that you may receive a lot of flutes, clarinets, and trumpets that need cleaning and some repair. You may also receive a variety of electric guitars and basses. In addition, there will likely be an accordion and a variety of electric keyboards. If you are hoping for nylon-string classical guitars, they might be the least of donations you receive. If this idea appeals to you, consider implementing it and arranging a swap with band or orchestra directors for instruments you can't use (instruments in exchange for volunteer help, perhaps?). If not, be specific about what you are willing to take. You may want to have a *guitar drop-off day*.

GoFundMe

Perhaps receiving used band instruments does not appeal to you, because your program simply needs cash. If you are teaching mariachi, for instance, you are aware how expensive the uniforms can be. If you are teaching handbells looking to add an octave to your handbell ensemble, the cost of one of the larger bells can be very pricey. GoFundMe.com has helped countless music programs achieve their goals. It is easy to use. You will need to write a compelling story explaining why you need the money and how it is going to be used. Include how many students it will impact and in what ways. There are many success stories of music programs reaching their financial goals and being able to purchase what they need for their students by using GoFundMe.com.

10

Websites and Documentation

In a poll of a total of one hundred selected high school guitar teachers (two teachers from each state), respondents were asked if their guitar program had a dedicated website. Only two responded with "yes." This same poll indicated that 68 percent of these teachers were teaching music classes other than guitar, such as band, choir, and orchestra. Many of the band programs in this survey group, on the other hand, did have dedicated websites. Other schools had only one website for the entire music department, which sometimes downplayed guitar and other innovative music ensembles in favor of more traditional, larger, or longer-established ensembles.

This example reveals that many guitar programs and other innovate ensembles are lagging in a website presence when they are compared to more traditional programs. A dedicated website is an important tool for outreach, engagement, and documentation, but there are many other ways to document your program and highlight its achievements to students, parents, and administrators. Communication is a big part of building an award-winning program. This chapter focuses on the importance of communicating through websites, teacher documentation, and student documentation; explains why they matter; and discusses how teachers can best document and publicize their programs and progress.

Maintaining and Promoting Your Website

Every school and school district has policies about websites. Some schools expect teachers to maintain a website for their individual programs. As a result, these schools may have separate websites for programs such as mariachi, jazz band, choir, orchestra, band, piano, and guitar. Other schools maintain only one website for the entire music department with links to the individual programs. Whatever your school's expectations are, teachers should always keep their program website pages up to date.

Building an Award-Winning Guitar Program. Bill Swick, Oxford University Press. © Oxford University Press 2022.
DOI: 10.1093/oso/9780197609804.003.0010

Typically, websites for music programs have photos of students and include information like audition requirements, a course handbook, course expectations, a performance calendar (including after-school rehearsals), travel information, uniform information, links to performance videos, links to recordings, awards, office hours, and teacher contact information. The main purpose of these websites is often to serve as a go-to resource for students and parents.

Before adding photos or videos of students, please be mindful of your school district's rules and guidelines related to media release forms and publicity release waivers (See Appendix D for more details). Also be aware of copyright laws as they apply to posting recorded or video student performances. As a word of caution, do not post any copyrighted printed music on your website for any reason unless you are the legal holder of the copyright.

Remember, however, that *anyone* can visit these sites. Websites can also be a way of networking and sharing resources and ideas with other teachers. A music teacher may be asked to teach a guitar class at school and have no idea how to get started. That teacher might begin by visiting websites created by other guitar teachers to see examples of other teachers' course expectations and class handbooks. The teacher may also watch performances hosted on the website to get ideas, for example, about music selection, uniforms, setup, types of guitars to use, sound reinforcement, and sitting arrangements. Watching other school programs performing can be a real learning resource for teachers and students alike.

If you wish to maintain an award-winning guitar program, start a dedicated website if your school allows, or push for a specific landing page on the school website. There is a practical as well as psychological reason for doing so. Depending on the region of the country, a high percentage of guitar students typically do not participate in other kinds of group extracurriculars, and guitar class is often the first opportunity for some students to be exposed to collaborative learning and teamwork. Belonging to an organization that is large and important enough to have its own website makes guitar class feel even more significant. Additionally, most secondary school students spend a significant portion of their lives online. Students can use the website to share recordings of past performances with their friends during lunch. If the program website maintains a gallery of photos, students may share those photos with friends as well.

A website is also handy when you need to explain your program in limited print. In these instances, providing the URL to the program's website will get a good deal of mileage. If people want to know more about the program, they can simply read more online. These links are helpful in bios, blogs, social media, printed articles, or anything else that has limited print space or word count, and of course providing links has the added benefit of increasing your website traffic. Printing the URL in performance programs is another way to send traffic to your site. Similarly, consider including the URL in your electronic signature in all emails. It is even possible that your website will be found by educational organizations that will link from their (typically) higher-traffic sites to yours, if they deem that it is a good resource for music education. All this is great publicity for your program.

In summary, websites make it possible for those outside of your immediate community of students and parents to find your program. Community groups may be looking for entertainment. Music educators may be looking for models for organizing a new music program already in place. Neighboring schools or districts may be looking at your program as a template for starting new programs. There are many reasons for starting and maintaining a website specific to your program. When designing your website, go for a simple look with high-quality photos and ample links that demonstrate the many facets of your program. Here are a few examples:

https://www.uncsa.edu/music/guitar/high-school-guitar.aspx
https://www.interlochen.org/music/academy/guitar
https://providencehall.com/high-school-guitar-program
http://teacherpress.ocps.net/christopherperez/fhs-guitar-course-syllabi

Documenting Your Accomplishments

When you are building an award-winning music program, it is important to be able to recognize any and all outstanding accomplishments. No one is going to document your successes and/or the successes of your students unless you do. Adding performances and awards to your website is one way to document success, but there are other methods and criteria for success as well. Create a file or folder on your computer for your successes and be vigilant about updating this information throughout the year. It does not matter how large or how small the accomplishment seems: write down the date when it happened, note whom it involved, and describe it.

An accomplishment may not be apparent unless you are looking for it. Jayson Martinez, an outstanding music educator from New Jersey, teaches at a high school that has 95 percent free or reduced breakfast and lunch, with a graduation rate of approximately 72 percent. Martinez discovered that students enrolled in a guitar class had a graduating rate of 90 percent or above, an approximately 20 percent higher rate than the student body total. This is a huge accomplishment! Yet it would have gone mostly unnoticed if Martinez had not tracked his students' performance beyond music class. And more importantly, Martinez documented his discovery, making it public not only to his school officials, but also to the entire Internet.[1]

An observation like this needs to be publicized and should be celebrated. Not only does it highlight the accomplishments of this particular group of students, but it also offers a strong argument for the impact of music education beyond the music classroom. Such accomplishments should be documented in your folder and shared as often as possible.

Oftentimes, *how* you document or publicize students' success is as important as the success itself. For example, say that a new high school guitar program in its first year sent students to participate in the MEA Solo and Ensemble Festival. At this particular festival, there were fourteen guitar students total who received blue ribbons and qualified to compete at the next level. Thirteen of these students were from this new program. To simply document that thirteen students received blue ribbons may be impressive but lacks full context. If, however, you document that 93 percent of all guitar students in the state qualifying for the next level were from the newly created program, it becomes clear this is quite a feat.

It is also important to document any time an ensemble performs in the community. At the end of the year, administrators will often ask how many hours you spent in providing service in a given community. All community performances count. Documenting throughout the year makes it easier to keep track of community hours and public performances. It is also impressive to have all performances listed for an end-of-year report.

Making recordings of student performances is also a form of documentation (and might also be a fundraising opportunity). Performance recordings today do not have the appeal they once had, as online streaming has made the market for CDs and other forms of purchasable recorded music much smaller, but for a school program, the recordings are a way to document history and are still important to do. Consider making a performance recording of the students in your program. Encourage your students to come up with an album cover, a set list, a title, the artwork, and the layout. Make this a collaborative project. Be mindful of the costs of making this recording and keep expenses to a minimum, simply because there is little chance the costs will be recouped through sales. It may be possible to attach the recordings to your program website and make the album free to stream. When the project is complete, remember to document it as an accomplishment for this year in your designated folder. Again, do not be shy about sharing this project with your administrative team. In preparation of making a public recording, make certain students are performing public domain music, original music, or music in which you are the legal copyright holder. Another option is to contact each publisher or composer and request permission to record and publish their music. Request all permissions to be done in writing and keep the correspondence in a safe location.

Apply to participate in a festival. In the event that your group is accepted, and your school approves the travel, make sure to document participating at a festival as one of this year's accomplishments.

Individual student accomplishments should be documented as well. It is common for music students to graduate from high school as valedictorian or salutatorian. These are major achievements. If one of your students is honored with this recognition or similar kinds of academic achievement awards, do not be shy about mentioning them as accomplishments for your program. Document any student award a student receives during the year whether it is directly related to your program or not. It is important to establish that your program attracts outstanding students, but students will also appreciate that you care about and celebrate their achievements outside of the music classroom.

Celebrate and document your own accomplishments as well. Directors should consider applying for the opportunity to speak or present at national conferences. This is a way to receive national attention for your contributions to music education. Applications for major conferences are usually due ten months or more before the event. If the time comes that you are selected to make a presentation at a conference, make sure to document this achievement in your annual report. Do not be shy about sharing this information with your administrative team.

Writing an article on a specific topic in music education is a great way to get published in an online blog or in a printed magazine or journal. Document each time you get something published and make certain that your administrative team is aware of your accomplishments. Add this publication to your program's accomplishments.

Apply for grants related to your program's interest. Many music-related grants are created to support the innovative ensembles. Do a little digging, find something related to what you are doing with your students that you could do even better if you had extra money, and apply. In the event you are awarded a grant, make sure to share that information with your administrative team and document it in your folder.

As a teacher, you may be recognized as teacher of the month, teacher of the year, or chili-cook-off champion. Include all of your awards as a part of your program's accomplishments; don't leave anything out! It is better to over-document, because as at the end of the school year you can read over your list of accomplishments and remove anything that no longer seems important. Share your list on your website and print it in the last concert program for the school year. You may even send this list to your administrators. Do not be shy when it comes to promoting your achievements and the achievements of your students. Sell your program as an award-winning program that students and parents can be proud of and want to be a part of.

Year-End Report

Few administrators request that teachers file a year-end report of accomplishments. Even if your administrators do not require a year-end report, however, I highly recommend preparing one. No one likes extra work, but the documentation is worthwhile. Over time you will forget the details of one year from another. A clear record of year-end reports is a quick reference if you need to be reminded of which students were enrolled in your classes, what music you performed, what trips you took, and what awards you may have won. If you are good at documenting events as they happen, assembling the year-end report will not take a great deal of time.

Part of each year-end report should include a complete listing of all students who were enrolled at the beginning of the year, in alphabetical order and listed class by class. You will likely create this document early in the school year. You should also document all trips and every performance and include the date, location, and reason for performing. This should be an on-going report and information and events added as they happen.

During the year, you or someone helping you will most likely be responsible for creating a performance program. On the program will be the date, time, and location of the performance, along with a listing of all students performing. In addition, there will be a complete listing of all of the music performed, in order of performance, including the names of the pieces, composers, and arrangers. Make sure to keep an electronic copy of this information in your dedicated folder for the year.

Another section of the year-end report should include an inventory listing of any new products purchased for the program, including instruments, accessories, sound equipment, and music. You should keep a tally at the end of the total expenditure and maintain an ongoing document that you add to when products are purchased. Do not wait until the end of the year to create this information; you should enter it as it happens.

The one document that will need to wait until the end of the year will be any year-end awards that are given to students and faculty. Some programs have an award ceremony at the end of the year to award students for being, for example, the most outstanding, the most improved, or the most likely to become a music teacher. The director may receive an award from professional colleagues or the administration. You should document all of these awards.

Near the end of the year, it is just a matter of putting these documents together into one year-end report. Imagine having a comprehensive document that contains the following:

1. An alphabetized listing of all students in each class from the first week of school
2. A listing of all performances and trips
3. A chronological listing of performance programs for the school year
4. An inventory of all new products purchased for the program and total expense
5. A listing of all awards presented to students and director in the program

If nothing else, create a PDF file of this document and keep it in your records. Make an additional file of just the annual accomplishments. This will be an easy file to share with your administrative supervisor, place on the program's website, and print in the final performance program of the school year. Do not share student names or school expenditures on your website.

Document with Photos

One of the best ways to document a school year is through photography. Photograph your students through the school year. There should be photos for each performance during the year, each trip, and any special events. You can use these photos for your website, for your YouTube channel, on performance programs and CD covers, in articles, and for whenever you need a photograph of your groups.

Encourage your students and parents to take many pictures of performances, trips, and award ceremonies as well. Chances are that they are already doing so! Set up a Google Share folder in Google Classroom for parents and students to share their photos. It is common for the administrator in charge of activities to request photos of your students performing music. Many times, the administration uses student photos on the cover and pages of the yearbook, in school pamphlets, in school brochures, on posters, and in a host of other promotional material created for the school. Consider having a dedicated photo gallery on your program website. When you are recruiting new students, you will always find it helpful to have plenty of pictures of students performing and having fun in various activities.

Though each school will have its own guidelines, make certain that you have a signed publicity consent form for each student before posting photos in public places, particularly on the Internet (see Appendix D for more details). This reminder was also discussed in Chapter 3, in the section titled "Parent Consent."

My Four Years

If you are teaching high school and have a four-year program, it is possible that you will have students in your program for four full years. After their four years in your classroom, you will likely know these students well. When it comes time for these students to graduate, it is always nice if you can give them something to remember you by. *My Four Years* is a bound booklet or document that combines the past four Year-End Reports into one document intended to be distributed only to graduating seniors who have been in the program for four years. In this booklet or document, students can see the names of all of the other students who were part of the program, all of the music they performed publicly, descriptions of all of the trips they took, and reminders of all of the performances on and off campus in their four years of high school. It will be a great keepsake. If you are teaching middle school, you may do the same project and title it *My Three Years*. Elementary teachers can call *My Five [or Six] Years*.

In addition to the booklet, consider putting together a photo journal of your students' time in your program. This is also a great gift! You should have all of the photos that have been stored in Google Classroom or iCloud or a public drive for the past years, and it is just a matter of putting them in a slideshow and adding some music. The expense for these two projects is minimal, and students and their parents are often extremely appreciative to receive these souvenirs at the end of their graduating year.

If you want to make something even more personal to individual students, you must spend a bit more time and must plan from the very beginning of the program for the project to work effectively. At the beginning of the first year of the program during the first week of school, distribute a file folder to every student. Their only responsibility is to put their name on the file tab. In addition, they may decorate the file folder any way they would like. When the students have finished, collect all file folders and put them into alphabetical order. This folder is going to be the only folder you use for each student during their entire stay in your program.

I suggest administering pretests at the beginning of the year, to evaluate how much each student knows when they arrive in the program. The results of these pretests should go into each student's folder. Every test, every paper, and every assignment will be kept in this folder. At the end of four years, these folders will be absolutely full. The contents in these folders represent all of the work each student has done, such as written exams, student goals, research papers, and concert critiques. Collectively, each folder will tell a story and demonstrate everything each student has learned from the very first week to graduation. In addition to being given a *My Four Years* booklet and a file attachment to four years of photos, each student should receive their file folder to keep. Of the three items, the file folder tends to create the most emotions. Students are very appreciative that their lives have been documented for the entire time they have spent in high school. They have certainly forgotten a big part of it already. It is these documents and photos that help retain the memories.

11

Building a Curriculum

Every guitar teacher should have a vault. What does that mean? A vault contains the nuts and bolts of a successful music program. It doesn't matter what you call it. You might refer to it as your Bag of Tricks or your Treasure Trove of Ideas. You may just call it your Curriculum, your Course Expectations, or the Program Sequence. The name itself is not important. The core idea is that you *have* a vault that contains the step-by-step procedure for taking a class of absolute beginning musicians and turning them into musical and expressive performers. This chapter details what the director of every award-winning guitar program should have in their vault, the teaching challenges they might face, and other practical tips for building a structure for successful learning and sustainable progress.

The Vault

Though the concept of a vault might sound obvious, this is the one element that separates those who have the potential to build an award-winning program and those who never will. The vault represents a carefully thought-out, purposeful approach that is key to any kind of success. Imagine that every music educator is an athletic coach. What makes a winning sports team? Ultimately, it's the game plan. Teams succeed when coaches prepare their athletes for competition and understand strategy. The content of your vault is your game plan. Music ensembles may not be as aggressive or competitive as sports teams, but music educators still need a game plan to prepare students for a performance and have a clear strategy for achieving excellence.

Your vault should contain step-by-step, tried-and-true methods to walk beginning students through the process of holding an instrument, reading music, and performing musically. You should have enough material in your vault to map out exactly what you will teach students as they progress from week to week. These materials consist of the literature, methods, pedagogy, and repertoire needed to create an award-winning music program for years

Building an Award-Winning Guitar Program. Bill Swick, Oxford University Press. © Oxford University Press 2022.
DOI: 10.1093/oso/9780197609804.003.0011

to come. In addition, you should have a well-defined timetable in which certain skills are introduced and when certain skills will be assessed.

It makes no difference what type of ensemble you are conducting or what style of music you are teaching. You must have a vault, and you must equip it with a clear procedure for how new students will be transformed into performers who can play musically and expressively. In addition, you might include plans to teach students how to be creative, how to compose, and how to improvise. None of these things will happen without a well-thought-out plan.

Some school districts require that teachers submit formal lesson plans. In these districts, administrators might like to see daily plans, or they might settle for weekly lesson plans. Even if your school district does not require you to prepare and submit formal lesson plans, I highly encourage creating and saving your weekly lesson plans anyway. The purpose of the lesson plan is to detail and document exactly what you will be teaching and what you expect students to learn in any given week. All of your lesson plans should be kept in your vault. Ideally, you should be so familiar with your curriculum that you could recite to an administrator what skills you will be teaching in any given week during the school year for each of the levels that you are teaching. To be able to do so requires well-written lesson plans and a deep understanding of the sequence of your plans. All of this preparation should be in the vault.

Just to be clear, the vault is a real thing, not something stored in your head. A logical place at school to store the vault would be in a dedicated drawer in a filing cabinet.

In addition to lesson plans, the vault should contain a copy of each of the method books that you will be using. You should have an in-depth knowledge of the contents of each method book and know how to model the techniques from these books. Modeling is particularly important, because students tend to have more respect for teachers who can do what they are asking the students to do. If it is important enough for your students to learn what you are teaching, then it is important enough for you to learn it as well and be able to model.

Don't be familiar only with the method books you will be using. Know exactly how many pages you plan to cover each week. You should have a clear idea where any given class should be at the end of the first quarter, at the end of the second quarter, and so on throughout the entire school year. Though some classes may move faster than others, and you can be flexible if needed, the idea is to have a clear goal marker for every class. That way, you can make sure that every student meets the goal markers set. This goal plan will be included as a part of your well-defined timetable.

The vault should contain well-thought-out music selections that reflect the techniques taught in the method books. If students can play six notes, you should have a library of pieces that can be performed with only those six notes. When students can perform eight notes, there should be more music to perform by using eight notes, and so on. This is called application. A good ratio of application to technique is to offer a pound of application for each ounce of technique. For instance, if the technique is introducing students to play eight notes, there should be twelve to sixteen songs using eight notes for students to apply this technique. Similarly, if students can play quarter notes and half notes (technique), there should be twelve to sixteen songs using those rhythms (application). Not providing enough application can be a downfall for many music educators. Technique is not truly learned until it can be demonstrated repeatedly through application. All this should be included in your lesson plans, which should document that you have thought out the content of your teaching materials down to what materials are intended to teach technique and what materials are intended for student application.

The vault should also contain your big-picture game plan. Just as a construction crew depends on a blueprint to build a structure, every music educator should have a blueprint for how to build an award-winning music program. A construction crew does not guess how many materials are needed, and a music educator should not be guessing, either. Create a blueprint for your program so that you know exactly what materials you need and in what quantity. This blueprint should clearly map out where everything belongs and what sequence to follow to make sure that the foundation is strong enough to support the structure. Without such a plan, your classes can go south quickly and certainly. Every music educator needs a blueprint for each class, and this should be in the vault.

If you are teaching intermediate- and/or advanced-level classes, performance repertoire should also be kept in the vault. Music educators need to have a clear understanding of student skills and the range of performance literature written to suit those skills. Selecting music that is beyond the skill level of the students can lead to frustration for all involved. This frustration might manifest in flaring tempers and critical comments, and no one benefits. Avoid this misfortune by having a clear understanding of the repertoire available that reflects current students' skill level. Appendix F: "Code for Level" has an easy-to-complete worksheet that should be filled out for every selection of music you are considering using. The five areas that require the most attention are time signature, key, highest note, most complex rhythm, and tempo. (See Appendix F.)

For part of the planning process, if the director knows of repertoire music that is written with an octave-and-a-half range within the playing knowledge of the students and uses rhythms that students are familiar with, the director should include a list of ensemble arrangements that can be performed with these defined skills. Students should be exposed to performing as an ensemble, large or small, as early as possible, and as frequently as possible.

Once students have developed enough skills to perform ensemble music, the director should have a defined list of musical terms to which students will be exposed in the process of rehearsing the music. From the very beginning, students should be taught the meaning of musical terms and how to incorporate these terms, and this instruction should be a part of every lesson plan and included as a part of the overall class blueprint. I have included a list of musical terms that I use with my students in Appendix G: "Musical Terms to Introduce during Rehearsal," but you can always add to this list as well. Make a habit of exposing students to five or more musical terms each week. This way, it will take about half a school year to introduce all of the terms listed. (See Appendix G.)

If you are teaching guitar for the first time and are not sure where to start in building your vault, the NAfME Guitar Council's standard practices is a good place to start. NAfME Guitar Council has a published "Guitar Best Practices" resource, a five-page document that provides, for the first four years of guitar education, a list of skills that should be taught each year in no particular order. (See Appendix B.)

Though this resource is a great starting point, remember that your teaching materials should reflect the organization of *your* school year. For those who teach a full-year guitar class, chances are that your school year is divided into four quarters and two semesters. Other schools, however, may divide the year into three equal parts. Organize exactly what will be taught and what materials will be covered in the first segment of the year, whether the first quarter or the first part of a three-part year. If you are teaching an intermediate or advanced level, you will also want to have a repertoire list aligned with the content of what is being taught. Do the same for each quarter or part of the school year and follow it.

Some professional arrangers and publishers write arrangements that are coded for skill level. If you decide to follow the NAfME Guitar Council's Best Practices, for instance, there are publishers who clearly label their guitar music as "Year One, Quarter Three," or "Year Three, Quarter One." In fact, there is a whole host of ensemble arrangements that are designed to be used for each quarter of a four-year guitar program. Using this material can save time and produce excellent results. Two such publishers to consider are www.GuitarintheClassroom.com and www.JWPepper.com.

The better organized you are and the better the blueprint you have, the greater chance you will have at building an award-winning music program. At no point should you be wondering what you are going to teach next. If you find that you are not clear on what you are teaching at all times, your vault is missing pieces of the puzzle.

Depending on the type of ensemble you are teaching, and the instruments involved, be mindful that each instrument has an established set of études or studies that have been collectively published and used by pedagogy experts. Once students are at the skill level to perform these études, your vault should include level-appropriate, sequenced études for each instrument that you teach. Students should be expected to learn one étude weekly or biweekly as part of their grade in your class. This exercise does not necessarily take up a lot of class time if you are using a musical application that stores the études and assesses student performances. Examples of this software are www.SmartMusic.com and www.MusicProdigy.com. Making the études a part of your program will strengthen students' abilities to read music and improve technique. These acquired skills will become apparent in ensemble performances. Having weekly or biweekly grades will also provide an accurate assessment of each student at the end of each quarter.

There are many things that music teachers should put in their vault but there is one thing that should *not* be there: free time! Teachers are more effective when they are actually teaching—that is, having the attention of the students and exposing them to elements about music they did not previously know. In my experience as an educator, asking students to break out into free time is not useful; "free time" might as well be called "waste time." There are optics to consider as well. How are you going to explain to an administrator what your students are doing if your supervisor walks into your classroom during "free time"? Nothing much good comes from free time in the music classroom. Teaching bell to bell is always the best policy. If you do not have enough materials to fill a normal class period, then make sure that next time, you are better prepared. The amount of information related to music is so vast and the number of days is so limited in all four years of high school to share and discuss all of that knowledge with students that how could there possibly be time for "free time"?

I Wrote My Own

Music educators will sometimes not find a method book that presents the materials exactly the way they would like. In some cases, this situation might mean that they need to spend more time in auditioning method books, but it could mean that they should alter their approach to teaching to better match a well-respected method. Unlike with band, choir, and orchestra, the teachers of the innovative ensembles—particularly guitar teachers—tend to write their own method books. Though there are currently many more band programs in the United States than guitar programs, the guitar method books in print far outnumber band method books. Given the number of new guitar method books published every year, you would think a guitar teacher could find a compatible method book. Yet during a brief survey of sixty-two classroom guitar teachers in the Clark County School District, it became clear that few teachers agree on using the same method books. Instead, the overwhelming response was that each teacher had either written a new method or revised an existing method. In some situations, teachers were using a combination of two or three existing method books that they blended in their own unique way.

The mix of method books poses challenges for guitar students who leave one school and transfer to another. If methods differ drastically from teacher to teacher, chances are slim that a transferring guitar student will be able to make the transition smoothly. This issue of difference from school to school has been partially addressed in other subjects as part of the Common Core philosophy. Following this philosophy, some school districts offer a standard method or textbook that teachers should use in the classroom so that, for example, all freshman English classes are presented with and learning from the same materials. For guitar classes and innovative ensembles, however, a district is not likely to decide on a required method, so teachers have a choice. Especially for those teachers who do not play guitar themselves, it can be daunting to go through and familiarize yourself with the vast number of materials that are available. Finding a good method can be challenging.

When guitar teachers post a question like "what is a good beginning guitar method book to use in class?" in a social media group of other school guitar teachers, the responses they receive are almost always the same: dozens of suggestions, each with a different recommendation.

Instead of wading through a sea of recommendations, consider spending time in seeking out successful award-winning programs. Ask and figure out who the leaders of guitar education are in your area and then consult those leaders. To build your own award-winning program, you should speak to and seek advice from someone who has already succeeded in creating such a program. See if they might be open to a mentor/mentee relationship so that you can benefit from their experiences. Copy what worked and learn from your mentors' mistakes. You may be surprised how willing others are to assist.

Sequencing

If you really can't find a method book that suits you, there may be another solution: sequencing, the art of rearranging the order in which materials are introduced. Some guitar teachers, for example, believe that it would be much better to teach the sixth string first, as opposed to starting with the first string. Not many method books in print (maybe none at this point) begin by teaching the sixth string, but almost every method book teaches the sixth string at some point. Sequencing might mean using a method book that starts with the first string, but in your lesson plan, week one will begin on page twelve (or whatever page the notes on the sixth string are introduced) instead of page one.

Another common example for guitar teachers is teaching chords. Some teachers teach chords before teaching note reading. If your method book teaches note reading first, consider starting your class on the page in the method book that introduces the chords you think should be taught first. Simply notate the page number in your weekly lesson plans. Method books do not have to be used in a numeric sequence. It is up to the teacher to decide in which order to introduce materials.

Rob Goldsmith, an outstanding guitar teacher in Las Vegas, Nevada, is a master at sequencing materials, as well as blending multiple texts. Goldsmith has become well known among his peers for his careful and precise sequences, and he is generous enough to print and share his sequences for the entire school year so that other guitar teachers can use them. Sequencing can be extremely effective. Goldsmith has led multiple award-winning middle school guitar programs, and takes pride because he did not spend a great deal of time in writing new materials. Instead, he found effective ways to use materials that were already in print.

When You Fail to Plan

Benjamin Franklin is known for his quotation, "If you fail to plan, you are planning to fail." This adage is recited regularly in education, often as a way to communicate to teachers the importance of writing lesson plans and having a clear direction for steering students from one level of skill to another. All teachers need to plan for how and when to introduce new materials, and how and when to make assessments to demonstrate that students are learning. I share this quotation here to reiterate the need to have a vault filled with pedagogy, methods, application, assessments, repertoire, defined timelines, and—perhaps most importantly—lesson plans. A teacher without lesson plans is like a builder without blueprints. Much is left to chance. Reading that second part of Benjamin Franklin's quotation should remind you that not having these elements in your planning will lead to imminent failure.

How Do You Know Your Students Are Learning?

This question may seem like an odd one to ask (for a teacher, it is usually pretty obvious when your students are learning) but it has become a more popular one in recent years. Being able to measure student learning in quantifiable ways is important to administrators, who may use this information to assess your effectiveness as an educator. They want to know if you can prove that your students are truly learning the contents of what you are teaching.

For a music educator, proving that your students are learning might seem like a pointless exercise. For instance, when beginning students entered class at the start of the year, they could not play a single note. Now listen to them as they get closer to the end of the year. They are obviously learning.

This answer will not be sufficient for most administrators, who want to see quantifiable student growth and how you are gathering that information. They know that your students are learning to perform on an instrument and are getting better, but at what percentage have they improved from two weeks ago? This is when the answer gets more complicated.

Earlier in this chapter, I mentioned using a set of études or studies carefully sequenced by skill level for weekly or biweekly playing exams. I also suggested using electronic applications like Smart Music or Music Prodigy as an easy way to offer regular grades and assessment. These apps, however, can also provide hard data to help you answer the question, how do you know your students are learning?

Here is one idea: assign your students a study in Smart Music or Music Prodigy with a clear due date. Since students tend to improve if they practice a little every day, as opposed to practicing a longer period just one day a week, you might add some structure to the assignment by requiring that every student perform a minimum of ten times and at least two times a day for a total of five days. Allow your students to perform the assigned study as many times as they would like until they receive their desired grade. Smart Music and Music Prodigy will record each performance and provide students a grade for each. As the teacher, you can see which days students log in, how long they practice, how many times they perform a study, and the scores they receive each time they perform. You can easily compare these scores to see the lowest, highest, and the range of scores in between.

If you regularly use these apps, gathering hard data on student growth is just a matter of calculating the percentage between the highest score and the lowest score to get the percentage of student growth each week. A student may have received a 40 percent as the lowest score of the week and an 80 percent as the highest score. In this case, the student demonstrated improvement by 100 percent. Though some might view this student as a B student for receiving only 80 percent, it is important to note that the student also doubled the lowest score, which demonstrates significant personal improvement or growth. Using these tools makes it very easy to show individual student growth on a regular basis.

Just One Percent a Day

Earlier in this chapter, I stressed the importance of having a big-picture blueprint for your classes and weekly lesson plans for your vault. If you are going to build an award-winning program, however, you also need to set daily goals. Start simply: do everything possible to improve by 1 percent a day.

That goal may sound ridiculous, but it works. Most school years are based on 180 days of instruction: hence, if you improve just 1 percent on where you were at the beginning of the year each day, near the middle of the school year your program will be nearly 100 percent as good as it was on day one— or, twice as good. By the end of the school year, that number will be nearly 200 percent, or four times as good. That is significant improvement in just one school year! Make sure that your students are also aware of their progress. When students recognize how much they have improved, they get excited, and the momentum continues.

How do you know if you are 1 percent better? That question is easy to answer if you teach and reteach. For example, on Monday, you might introduce a one-octave major scale in the key of C major. You also introduce two chords in first position and spend most of the class period in making sure every student is playing these chords correctly. Every day for the rest of the week, you are going to reteach the very same information, with the expectation that as you cover the material again, your students will do slightly better and learn faster each time. On Tuesday, for example, there might be a few minutes at the end of the period to introduce application for these new skills. On Wednesday, you will again reteach the lesson and there should be even more time left for more application. By Friday, or the fifth day, students should be much faster than they were on Monday and there will be even more time left at the end of the class to introduce applications of what you are teaching. For example, you may demonstrate how to play a C chord followed by the C major scale and ending with the C chord. Have half of the class strum the C chord while the other half plays the scale, and then switch. Be creative in finding ways to apply the content of each week's lessons and add a little more application toward the end of each class as the week progresses.

The main idea here is this: don't try to make radical changes in a short amount of time because doing so can often lead to discouragement. Instead, every day make small improvements that will gradually result in the change you want. Each day, just focus on getting 1 percent better in whatever it is you are trying to improve. That's it. Just 1 percent. It might not seem like much, but those improvements will start compounding. At the beginning, your improvements will be so small as to seem practically nonexistent, but gradually and ever so slowly, you will start to notice just how much your students have progressed. Be aware of what cannot be easily changed. Do not spend time tackling things you cannot control or issues that will not budge. For example, you may have a student who is not interested in learning, will not participate, or has completely given up. You may have another student who believes their fingers are too fat, and another who thinks their fingers are too short. Spending class time on these issues is not productive. Find time to tackle these issues privately. Instead, focus on the small things that can be changed and make a small improvement every day. It is amazing what can be accomplished over time.

There Are No Bs in Music

The title of this section can be interpreted in a lot of ways. Some might read this to mean that all students want and should get As in music class—and there are teachers who do subscribe to that philosophy and consistently give every student in their class an A grade. This philosophy certainly simplifies the grading process for the teacher and lowers the number of parent complaints and parent conferences. This way, everyone is happy. Students like to get As, parents like to see them, and teachers make their own lives easier. Giving everyone an A also makes the teacher look good. Every student succeeds, and so the teacher must be an effective educator.

Yet there is another way to read this statement, which is that there *should be* no Bs in music. The music teacher and their students must always deliver A-level performances. For instance, what would you do if you purchased a recording of your favorite musical artist and every fifth note on the recording was bad in some way? The pitch may be off. The rhythms may be wrong. The lyrics may be wrong. Whatever it is, every fifth note in some way is incorrect. That is how a B—or 80 percent accuracy—sounds in the audio spectrum. For a student to receive a B in music class means that student consistently misses every fifth note or performs 20 percent of all notes incorrectly 100 percent of the time. As a consumer of music, you would be disappointed if you paid for a recording that was only 80 percent accurate.

For a parent attending a school ensemble performance, it would be disappointing to hear mistakes being made 20 percent of the time. By grading standards, that performance might be a B, which is usually considered an acceptable grade in other classes. But if you observe an ensemble operating at 80 percent, chances are you would be quite critical of the director. If you had to assign a grade to such a director, it would probably be one lower than a B. Parents may tolerate seeing a B on a report card, but they will certainly be less tolerant of B performances. Similarly, no director would be happy if their ensemble missed every fifth note. Music educators strive for 100 percent accuracy 100 percent of the time. While we all know that perfection is perhaps unrealistic, we still believe in it. We also know mistakes are going to happen, but we do what we can to avoid as many mistakes as possible.

To build an award-winning music program, consider what you are willing to do to eliminate Bs in your classroom. Promote the concept of performing at 95 percent or higher (missing one note out of every twenty). While this is not perfection, it can be a goal. Performing at 95 percent accuracy deals just as much with attitude as it does with skill level. While attitude may not be something to keep in the vault, it is certainly something to share in the classroom. Encourage accuracy at all times and convince students that playing accurately is a possibility if they can visualize themselves doing so. Modeling accuracy is an important element of being a music educator. Remember, there are no Bs in the words "award-winning."

12

Teaching the Whole Student

Award-winning music programs usually have one thing in common: the director puts the students first. It is rare to find a successful music program that prioritizes competitions and constantly winning above all else. Long-term, award-winning programs are necessarily led by directors who think about students: their needs, their education, and the experiences they will have participating in their music program.

Some high school music directors teach class as if every student were going to college and majoring in music. The numbers, however, are not there to support this type of thinking. According to the College Music Society in an article published in January 2015 and titled "Facts and Figures Concerning Music and Higher Education in the United States," the percentage of high school music students who major in music in college is on average going to be approximately 10 percent.[1] That means 90 percent of the students in high school music classes are there to enjoy the current experience, not to intensely prepare for higher-education music programs. Think about what students really need, in the here and now. Even those who will go to college for music will have four or more years to learn what they need to learn at the college level; that is something for the future. And yes, of course you would like your students to be prepared for college, but your role is simply to make sure that the students who will be auditioning for college programs have the skills to be accepted. This is your main job as a high school music teacher: not to get your students playing at college level, but to make sure that all your students can pass a college entrance audition, especially if you know some are planning to attend college as music students.

As a high school teacher, you should be aware of college audition requirements (these are usually easily found online on the school website, by instrument: see Appendix H: "Sample College Audition Requirements"), but passing a college entrance audition is the end game, and only a small percentage of all seniors in your classes are going to be interested in auditioning. Think about preparing *all* your students for college, regardless of what their majors will be.

Building an Award-Winning Guitar Program. Bill Swick, Oxford University Press. © Oxford University Press 2022. DOI: 10.1093/oso/9780197609804.003.0012

If you are teaching middle school and live in an area that offers a magnet performing-arts high school, these concepts also apply. There will be audition requirements, and while only a small percentage of students will be interested in attending, there is still a need to prepare all of your students, even if you don't know which students may have an interest of continuing their music education.

What do students really need? According to Clint Page from familyeducation. com, here are the top ten skills that high school students need to be prepared to enter college.[2] (These skills may also apply to middle schoolers transitioning into high school.)

1. Time management
2. Good study habits
3. The ability to set attainable goals
4. Concentration
5. Good note taking
6. Completion of assignments
7. Review of daily notes
8. Organizational skills
9. Motivation
10. Commitment

Do these skills seem familiar? You could argue that they are needed for any kind of academic success. Whether you are a middle school teacher preparing your students for high school, or a high school teacher preparing your students for college, these are important skills to develop within your program. The takeaway from this chapter and the following sections is that directors of award-winning programs must teach the whole student to prepare them for success in all other areas of their lives.

Time Management

Most secondary schools consider music classes to be elective classes. Many schools distinguish between teachers who teach academic classes and those who teach elective classes. On many campuses, the two are even physically separated—the music classes may take place in a "arts" building, for example, and other classes in a "main" building—and it can be challenging for faculty members who teach academics to mingle with those who teach electives. This separation of "core" classes versus "electives" often leads to the belief that academic classes are more important. The content taught in academic classes is often the information students need to know when taking standardized tests, and the credits earned from the academic classes play an important role towards graduation.

Yet music students overall tend to do better in school than students who do not take music classes. As I mentioned earlier, one high school in New Jersey has data indicating that students enrolled in music classes have a 20 percent greater chance of graduating from high school than those who are not. One of the contributing factors of higher graduation rates may be tied to time management.[3]

Music classes are known for setting time limits and encouraging students to learn a piece of music by a certain day. One of the best lessons an award-winning director can teach students is how to manage their time to the point that they can practice music every day and complete homework assignments for all other classes with the focus of maintaining good grades in all classes, not just music class.

School counselors often give students tools like student planners or daily time management sheets with space to write down daily home-work, note when assignments are due, and block out time to complete assignments and tasks. Some students do better by using these types of tools. For a music teacher who recognizes students with time management issues, it becomes your responsibility to set up meetings with the students and counselors to assist them in getting the tools needed to improve time management.

Music directors often encourage music students to practice every day for fifteen minutes. Just fifteen minutes, but every day. Once students have reached this goal, add five minutes, and make it twenty minutes a day. Music students who practice daily will progress so much faster than those students who practice sporadically or not at all. Practicing daily eventually becomes a daily habit, which is a part of time management.

When discussing time management with music students, make certain that you are talking to the whole student. In other words, do not focus just on practicing music, but recognize that students attend several other classes and have homework in these classes as well. Encourage time management as it applies to the whole picture. This encouragement will be a gift that will last a lifetime.

Good Study Habits, Completion of Assignments, and Organizational Skills

Each of these qualities is important for student success. Parents sometimes report that their children spend all of their time in playing music and spend no time in studying. This is a problem. Though parents can encourage their children to study, sometimes it means so much more when the music director makes the same suggestion. When the music director inspires students to do better in other classes, students appreciate the support, the compassion, and the encouragement. This inspiration is important as a piece of building an award-winning music program. It is never just about the music, but always about the whole student.

Most teachers have access to a grade-book software that enables them to see not only how students are doing in their own classes, but also how students are doing in their other classes. One feature that most of the software programs have now is the ability to see any missing assignments a student may have in any class. Missing assignments are truly the enemy and the shortcoming that will bring a student's grade down the fastest. Music directors should have a "no tolerance attitude for missing assignments in any class by any student," which should be made clear at the beginning of the school year. Just having this policy will set a standard that music students should and will do better. When students are missing assignments, these cases need to be handled individually and may need to include a meeting with the parents, school counselor, and teacher who did not receive the assignment. Students should be aware that you will be looking and keeping an eye out for missing assignments in other classes, but you do so because you care about their future, you care about them, and you support them in doing their absolute best.

Some schools have strict eligibility guidelines in place already. For example, some schools have policies that prohibit students from traveling or participating in extracurricular activities if they receive a D or an F as a quarter grade in any class. This type of policy could have real, negative effects on your overall ensembles if students are sidelined due to poor or failing grades. This potential danger is another reason that it is so important to keep an eye on how well your students are doing in other classes and motivate students in doing well academically.

Goals Within Reach

Setting attainable goals should be part of every music class. It helps if the director creates an easy-to-follow worksheet that guides students in writing their goals for the first half of the school year. Students can fill out these worksheets during the first week of school. Encourage students to list five goals they would like to achieve by the end of the first semester. Explain that goals must be defined, must have a time limit, must be attainable, and should be measurable or assessable in some way so that it is obvious once the students have completed a goal.

At midterm, have students read their goals and make a personal assessment in terms of whether they have completed their five goals. Any goals not completed may be repeated for the remainder of the year. Students should replace the goals that have been completed and have five goals to work on for the remainder of the school year. At the end of the second semester, have students review this new set of goals and make an evaluation if they completed their goals or not. (See Appendix I: "Goals Within Reach.")

Good Note Taking and Reviewing Daily Notes

Some estimate that the freshman class of high schoolers in the year 2018 were one of the first groups of students who have had an electronic device in their hands since they were old enough to hold one. The official age range or year may vary, depending on whom you ask, but the point is that all K–12 teachers are now working with students equipped with these devices. The newer-generation students are a little different from the students who came before them. When a teacher is lecturing, these students ask themselves a simple question: is this information something I really need to know now, or is this something I can google later? The answer is always the same: google it if you need it later.

Sometimes students barely even bring pens and pencils to school with them, instead using laptops and other electronic devices. My experience suggests that note taking is just nonexistent with this demographic of students, and therefore a daily note review is not going to happen, simply because there are no notes to review. The format of a teacher lecturing and students taking notes may be something from the past. If you would like your students to have written information, it may be more efficient to type the information and attach it to your class program's website or put the information in Google Classroom or the software your school is currently using for communication purposes.

These student behavior trends are likely to continue as phones become faster, the Internet connections become faster, and world information continues to increase annually. Here is something to consider. According to the "Knowledge Doubling Curve" created by Buckminster Fuller in 1982, in the year 1900, human knowledge doubled every one hundred years. By 1945, human knowledge doubled every twenty-five years.[4] Authors Ray Kurzweil, Eric Schmidt, and Jared Cohen write in their book *The New Digital Age* that human knowledge is doubling every thirteen months and has the potential to do so in every twelve hours in the future.[5] Who has time for taking notes? By the time you get back to reading the notes, the information may have changed.

Concentration, Motivation, and Commitment

It is true that students who can concentrate tend to do better in school. With the increasing awareness and diagnosis of various forms of attention deficit disorders in young people, concentration is something that all teachers need to be mindful of when working with students; you should not assume that all students are the same when it comes to their ability to concentrate. For many students, concentration is simply not something that happens naturally. The study of music has been known to assist students with concentration, but the skills learned in music do not always transfer to other subjects.

One of the benefits of having students perform as an ensemble in music class is the opportunity for them to stay focused on playing their part while they are hearing other parts being played around them. This skill requires a great deal of concentration. Though it does not come easily to every student at first, most students eventually learn the skill when they are given the opportunity to do it every day. This type of concentration transfers to other forms of musical performance, such as solo playing or single-note studies. Overall, this is a good argument for including ensemble playing as a daily activity.

Motivation is another important element of an award-winning music program. A director should not assume that all students coming into their classroom will be motivated to learn. Motivating students to put in the work to learn to play and excel at a musical instrument is your responsibility. The end of Chapter 5 offered a list of ideas for how to motivate students, but remember that this is not a one-time consideration. Teaching the whole student means checking in regularly to make sure that your students continue to be motivated.

Commitment is another skill that students do not automatically bring into the classroom. Jim Rohn is credited for the saying, "Motivation is what gets you started. Commitment is what keeps you going."[6] Here is an anonymous saying that captures the meaning of commitment: "Commitment means staying loyal to what you said you were going to do long after the mood you said it in has left you."

Though concentration, motivation, and commitment are key to the success of a student, if you want your students to demonstrate these characteristics, someone has to demonstrate them all on a daily basis. A director of an award-winning music program will model these three skills and encourage students to "do as I do."

When beginning to learn to play a musical instrument, students find that most musical studies are only four measures in length. As the students progress, the exercises gradually become longer, extending to eight measures, then sixteen, and so on. The process of being able to start an exercise and play it in time for the length of sixteen measures is an example of learning the ability to concentrate. Students who are able to play thirty-two-measure exercises in time with minimum mistakes clearly are demonstrating concentration. For a teacher, modeling that you are able to do so is especially important. At the beginning of each week when there is a new weekly exercise, play it in class with a metronome and demonstrate that you are able to play the exercise while possibly talking about the piece as you are performing it.

I mentioned earlier that encouraging students to practice five days a week for fifteen minutes is far more beneficial than practicing one day a week for one or more hours. I also suggested using a software program like Smart Music or Music Prodigy that evaluates student performances and provides grades. Experience indicates that students are motivated to practice when each knows their highest score of the week in a music app counts as their weekly grade. As a teacher, you can promote motivation by making it possible for students to have total control of their grades that reflect their individual efforts.

Commitment may be the easiest to model. Simply show up, be in the classroom on time every day, and do what you say you are going to do. Strive for perfect attendance and always keep your word. It is difficult to encourage students to be committed when the teacher misses excessive school days and/or breaks promises. If commitment is what you want from your students, it is imperative to demonstrate your commitment as a teacher.

Characteristics of an Award-Winning Director

Modeling behavior is a key part of teaching and is especially important if you want to lead an award-winning program. A program cannot succeed if a director is not committed or motivated both in terms of developing their students and developing themselves. Following are some key characteristics of an award-winning director.

Good News Person

There are going to be times when you will need help or assistance from others. In a school environment, everyone is busy and it may seem that the only time you talk to someone is when you need a favor from them. This is not a healthy state or an effective way to develop good relationships with your colleagues.

Make a point of talking to others when you need absolutely nothing from them. Go out of your way to have positive conversations. Be careful not to complain or be overly critical and certainly do not speak poorly of others. Be the "Good News Person." This idea comes from Matt Denman, a well-known music educator, guitarist, composer, and businessman from Oklahoma City, Oklahoma. Denman regularly exudes the qualities of a Good News Person and is a good model to follow. People genuinely like him and want to spend time with him. Others want to study with him or hear him perform. They are anxious to hear his new compositions and, most importantly, they want to do business with him. Follow Denman's model and this could be you. If his name seems familiar, Denman was mentioned in Chapter 5 as a model university recruiter. His positive attitude is contagious, and it has proven very successful in attracting students to his programs.

How can you be a Good News Person? Do not be shy about sharing the many positive things that are happening with your students and your program. Share your joy for being at school and express your excitement for all of the opportunities that are being given to you. Be that person who makes people smile when you walk into the room. Be that person who is going to say something intelligent and in the most positive and entertaining manner. Be that person whom others want to be around and spend time with. When the day comes that you do need a favor from someone, they will more likely be happy to assist you and feel good about it. In exchange, demonstrate gratitude. Acknowledge their help and go out of your way to express your appreciation for their assistance.

School environments are notorious for breeding negativity and complainers. In many cases teachers feel overworked and underappreciated—and to add to that list, underpaid. It is easy to fall into a negativity trap. Keep out of that trap. Even if you are feeling underappreciated, do not succumb to the negativity, and especially do not let it seep into your relationship with students and peers. Be just the opposite. Bring joy into the lives of others. Be the person whom students want to hang out with. Have the classroom that is always filled with students before and after school and during lunch. Brag about your students and let others know you are proud of them. It is sometimes necessary to be negative with students privately, but consider the old adage, "Praise in public, criticize in private."

Firm, Fair, and Consistent

It is important to treat your students fairly, but just as important that your students believe that you treat them fairly. Getting feedback from students who say they believe you are fair is a real compliment. During this time of increased sensitivity to issues such as race and sexuality, particularly in schools, it is more important than ever to make it clear to students, parents, and peers that you are fair and treat all students the same. All students should have no doubt that they will receive fair treatment when it comes to grades, assessments, comments, and general conversations, regardless of such factors as their age, race, religion, and sexual identity.

Grades motivate most students, and the final grade of the quarter is important to them. Students must know that you are fair when it comes to grades, and the best way to do so is to have well-defined guidelines that clearly explain what is necessary to earn an A in your class. The guidelines should be so specific that students will easily understand why they have fallen short of a desired grade if and when they have.

In addition, it is important that your classroom has rules and guidelines to assure that disruptions are at a minimum and you are providing a safe and secure learning environment. To do so requires you be firm. In other words, you must insist that all students follow classroom guidelines at all times—whatever those guidelines may be. When students step out of line, you should be quick to say something and maintain order in your classroom.

Your students should know that you will call out any student who does not follow classroom guidelines. If you do so, the student involved should not be surprised by your actions. Students should not feel compelled to accuse you of singling out individuals, because classes have witnessed your consistency in the past.

Students should also be aware of consequences if they choose to step out of line. Your classroom handbook should have clear, precise definitions of misconduct and of the consequences for the most common types of bad judgment—for instance, when students are using their phones while in class for any reason not related to classwork. Any time they do so, consequences should follow the handbook, regardless of which student it is. At no time should the consequence for breaking a rule be greater than what is defined in the class handbook. At no time should a consequence be greater for one student than another. You must be consistent. Students should be aware that you are firm, fair, and consistent and have expectations that you will remain so.

Honesty

There is lot to be said about the old adage "honesty is the best policy." For music educators, giving playing assessments to students is a key part of the job. Although you should remain positive and always find something encouraging to say to a student, it is also important to be honest. Students need to feel that you are truthful with them about their skill levels. Doing so does not mean that you need to be critical, although some students may interpret what you say as such. There is a fine line between being constructively honest and being gratuitously critical, and sometimes they can be confused for each another. The most common observation of a student performance is lack of preparation. It is usually obvious when a student has not prepared (not put the time in for the week) compared to when they are struggling because the music is too difficult. Saying to a student that it sounds as if they had not worked on a piece that week is an honest observation that often leads to a reply admitting that there was no time that week because of conflicts. At that point, you may continue the conversation by saying that it will be necessary to repeat the same study for next week and you hope that there will be more time to prepare it.

On the other hand, after the same performance, the teacher may suggest that the piece is too hard for the student, or the student does not have the necessary skills to play the piece correctly. This suggestion would be unjustified criticism and does not foster encouragement. The student takes nothing useful from this type of comment. If indeed the student's skills are not quite equal to the task, then you should find a diplomatic way of suggesting a piece that is less challenging but still rewarding for a student with a certain skill level. Students who are accustomed only to praise may find your honesty hard to take at first. Over time, they will learn to appreciate it and respect you for it. The end result is that students will also learn to be honest with themselves and will be better equipped for self-assessment as they become more independent.

Dressing for Success

Many books have been written on the importance of dressing for success, but what that means has changed alongside social norms. An older book might advise male teachers to wear a jacket and tie to school daily, and female teachers nice dresses, skirts, or other tailored outfits. Those days are gone, and this perspective is now considered outdated. Teachers today rarely wear jackets and ties or dresses and skirts to school every day. So how does a teacher dress for success at a time when dress at schools has become so casual?

Dressing for success can have different meanings in different environments, but the key is to dress to show you are proud to lead your music program. If your school provides T-shirts or other apparel specific to the music program, wear those clothes proudly. If not, and you have the funds to do so, consider finding a local embroidery shop that will embroider your school logo with the name of your program and include a small emblem that represents your program. For example, if you are teaching guitar, have your school logo, school name, your title, and a guitar embroidered on the shirts that you would normally wear to school. Consider doing so on various colored polo-style shirts, solid-color dress shirts, a blouse, a vest, or a hoodie. Brand your program by wearing apparel that represents your program. Your students will appreciate that you think enough of their program to wear clothing that represents it.

If your school has an online merchandise shop on the school website, you may consider selling student-sized shirts with the same logo. Students in your program may like wearing these shirts as well.

Forgiveness

Being a music teacher requires thick skin. Chances are you are going to be criticized by students, parents, and your administration. During your career, you are likely to put your heart and soul into a project that you are most proud of, only to receive criticism from the least expected sources. It is going to happen, and it may happen many times during your career. People are likely to say the most hurtful things to you about your work or how you work and not even be aware how badly it hurts for you to hear it. To maintain a strong character and to be successful, you will need to learn the fine art of forgiveness.

In Luke 23:34, Jesus said, "Father, forgive them, for they do not know what they are doing." It can be very confusing when teaching school. Students are developing independence from their parents. As students start feeling more independent, they frequently say and do things that are hurtful, difficult, and disappointing to watch and hear. They frequently make bad choices. As their music educator, you may be the disciplinary adult in some of their lives, particularly while they are at school. There will be many opportunities to demonstrate empathy and understanding along with forgiveness.

Parents sometimes give their children too much independence during this time in life and start treating them more like adults because they are starting to look more like adults. But they are still developing adult emotions, thought processes, and social skills—and they frequently make bad choices.

To quote "Adolescent Maturity and the Brain: The Promise and Pitfalls of Neuroscience Research in Adolescent Health Policy" by Dr. Sara B. Johnson and colleagues, "The frontal lobes, home to key components of the neural circuitry underlying 'executive functions' such as planning, working memory, and impulse control, are among the last areas of the brain to mature; they may not be fully developed until halfway through the third decade of life."[7]

Thus children do not really become adults until their mid- to late twenties. Their filters for making good decisions do not develop until this age. So, you could say in jest that a fifteen-year-old is only "half baked." Teens are likely to say and do what is hard to hear and watch. Again, it is important to learn to forgive. Forgiveness does not mean to forget; rather, it is a deliberate decision to release feelings of resentment toward a person or group of people. Teaching can be a training ground for learning to get along with others and it requires a good deal of self-protection. Being able to forgive will come in handy as long as you are participating in the journey of public education.

If you are going to build an award-winning program, just be mindful that the more public your program becomes, and the more successful your program appears, the more criticism you will receive from a variety of people who do not have award-winning programs. There will be plenty of opportunities to practice forgiveness.

Music Classes, How Important Are They?

As an award-winning music educator, you are keenly aware that you want each of your students to do well in all of their classes. You are also mindful that only a small percent, 10 percent or less, are likely to go to college to study music. You look at each student as a whole being and are aware of their needs. You have a strong desire that each and every student will find success and happiness in life. You hope that each of your students remains a lifelong learner. You may also have the desire that your students will in some way keep music in their lives and be lifelong consumers of music. And yet you walk and talk as if your music program were the most important class on campus.

In some ways, it is. It is your class wherein your students will meet and maintain long-term friendships. It is your class wherein students get to travel, bond, create lifelong memories, and be exposed to places and experiences they would otherwise never see or have. It is your class wherein students learn discipline and the expectation of high standards. It is your class wherein students learn time management, motivation, and commitment. It is your class wherein all students are treated equally, fairly, and consistently, regardless of age, sex, or race.

You clearly do not believe your music classes are the most important on campus. You do not believe that for a minute, and yet you promote your program as if it were. Though administrators would never openly admit it, if you are not putting your program as the number-one most important aspect on your campus, they really do not want you. No one wants a leader who thinks their program has less merit than others. Administrators want teachers who are going to fight for and defend their programs. Administrators want music educators who put their programs first, put their students' needs first, and put the fight for equality and representation first.

Does this attitude make you appear conceited or self-centered to other teachers? It may. That is certainly not an image you would like to portray, but yes, you could appear that way to others. However, if you are going to build an award-winning program, it is difficult to do if you honestly believe that all other classes are more important and should come first, and your program should be considered only after all others. After all, if your program is not important to you, why should it be important to your students?

Be mindful of all of the good that comes from teaching music to students, and all of the good that comes from participating in an ensemble, such as teamwork and collaboration. Know that when your current students are at their fiftieth high school graduation reunion, they will still remember your name, the trips they took, and the fun they had while being in your program.

Empathy Leading to Leadership

Empathy means being able to understand the needs of others. It means you are aware of the feelings of others and possibly aware how they are thinking or what is on their minds. You have the ability to recognize, understand, and feel the emotions of other people. For a teacher, being able to apply your empathy to students will go a long way. What does empathy have to do with leadership? According to Lolly Daskal, author of *The Leadership Gaps*, leadership is about having the ability to relate to, connect with, listen to, and bond with people for the purpose of inspiring and empowering their lives.[8] According to Daskal, here are six ways empathy can assist you in becoming the best leader you can be:

1. Empathy creates bonds.
2. Empathy creates insight.
3. Empathy teaches presence.
4. Empathy guides understanding.
5. Empathy sharpens people skills.
6. Empathy cultivates a better communicator.

For a music educator of an award-winning program, demonstrating empathy with your students is a must. Empathy gives you a greater awareness of the needs of your students. It allows you to create an environment of open communication with your students and provides for more effective feedback. Empathy can make educators more aware of what problems students are dealing with and thus may lead to a resolution. Students tend to gravitate to the teachers who understand them, are open with them, and spend time asking questions that assist in supporting communication. Students tend to do better in classes in which the teacher is regularly empathetic. To do and be so, avoid making accusations, pointing fingers, and/or placing blame on students. Instead, be open, ask questions, and give students an opportunity to explain what they are feeling or what they are dealing with. In many cases, students can be grappling with some heavy issues that affect them emotionally, physically, and/or psychologically, and the challenges they face may shock you. Take the time to ask. Take the time to show interest. Be a good listener. Developing empathy with your students will make you a better teacher.

As a general rule, if your music class is an hour in length, tell yourself that the one hour each day that your students spend in your classroom will be the best hour of their day. And then, make certain that it is.

Conclusion

By now, you are either motivated to build an award-winning music program or not. It is possible that you have already built such a program and just received confirmation by reading this book. No matter where you are in the process, I hope that the contents of this book have provided a clear image of the many moving parts involved in creating and managing an award-winning program.

Many of the skills required to build an award-winning music program were not offered while you were in college and preparing to be a music educator. Elisa Janson Jones says it best in her article, "7 Things They Don't Teach Music Education Majors (That You'll Wish They Had): "as much as I knew about teaching music, there was a lot I didn't know about how to run a music program."[9] She continues by listing seven business skills that every music educator needs to learn: email communication, marketing, salesmanship, financial planning, problem solving, diplomacy, and web mastery.

Many of these business skills have been covered in this book. And yes, running an award-winning music program requires business skills, people skills, leadership skills, and of course musical skills. Building an award-winning music program requires checking many different boxes. It is a process, and it does not happen overnight. It is a commitment, a vision, and a dream. First and foremost, it is for the students whose lives will be touched by the experience.

Trophies and accolades are there as reminders of the outstanding performances by your program as its leader. The real rewards are knowing that you have done everything possible to provide the absolute best music education experience possible to the many young lives that have crossed and will in the future cross your path.

Qualities of an Effective Music Educator

Self-Reflection Quiz

Circle Y for Yes and N for No

Y N 1. I possess a legitimate love for music.

Y N 2. I possess strong communication skills and am an excellent communicator.

Y N 3. I love technique and theory and know how to sell them to students.

Y N 4. I have a clear understanding of student capabilities.

Y N 5. I choose appropriate learning materials and musical selections.

Y N 6. I have strong organizational skills.

Y N 7. I believe that every child can learn to play music and reach their full potential.

Y N 8. I think of myself as a patient teaching.

Y N 9. I am passionate about teaching and working with students.

Y N 10. I assist students in becoming independent and creative.

Y N 11. I teach and promote strong sight-reading skills.

Y N 12. I can spot issues quickly and provide instant solutions.

Y N 13. I am constantly learning new things and am a good model.

Y N 14. I create lessons with objectives, targets, and assignments.

Y N 15. I am creative at explaining things for various types of learners.

Y N 16. I get to know each student and connect with them.

Y N 17. I am not afraid to introduce challenging things in class.

Y N 18. I include fun and joy whenever possible.

Y N 19. I possess and demonstrate confidence.

Y N 20. I have and maintain a strong work ethic.

Each statement may be used as a daily mantra or affirmation. Read each statement and circle Y if you believe you are doing these things, and N if you think you need more work in this area. Count the circled Ns when you are complete. Four Ns is an 80 percent. Two Ns is a 90 percent. Focus on the statements in which you respond with an N.

NAfME Council for Guitar Education Guitar Best Practices

Years 1, 2, 3, and 4

Many schools today offer guitar classes and guitar ensembles as a form of music instruction. While guitar is a popular music choice for students to take, many teachers offer instruction for which guitar is their secondary instrument.

The NAfME Guitar Council collaborated and compiled lists of Guitar Best Practices for each year of study. They comprise a set of technical skills, music experiences, and music theory knowledge that guitar students should know through their scholastic career.[1]

As a Guitar Council, we have taken careful consideration to ensure that the lists are applicable to middle school and high school guitar class instruction, and may be covered through a wide variety of method books and music styles (classical, country, folk, jazz, pop). All items on the list can be performed on acoustic, classical, and/or electric guitars.

NAfME Council for Guitar Education

Best Practices Outline for a Year One Guitar Class

YEAR ONE—At the completion of year one, students will be able to:

1. Perform using correct sitting posture and appropriate hand positions
2. Play a sixteen measure melody composed with eighth notes at a moderate tempo using alternate picking
3. Read standard music notation and play on all six strings in first position up to the fourth fret
4. Play melodies in the keys C major, a minor, G major, e minor, D major, b minor, F major and d minor
5. Play one octave scales including C major, G major, A major, D major and E major in first position
6. Have a tonal range which extends to the A above the staff
7. Identify chord diagrams and play major, minor and dominant seventh chords in first position in the keys of C major, G major, D major, d minor, A major, a minor, E major, and e minor
8. Strum rhythms to include whole, half, quarter and eighth notes including simple syncopation
9. Play power chords using roots on open sixth, fifth and fourth strings
10. Read and understand symbols indicating up and down strokes using a pick, also known as alternate picking
11. Play arpeggios in a finger-style style as an accompaniment

12. Identify and use p-i-m-a [p = pulgar (thumb), i = indice (index finger), m = medio (middle finger), a = anular (ring finger)] including rest stroke (apoyando) and free stroke (tirando)
13. Improvise a melodic line to a simple two or three chord progression such as the blues using a pentatonic or blues scale
14. Identify and name the parts of the guitar
15. Identify basic musical symbols
16. Tune the guitar by pitch matching
17. Play effectively and dependably as a part of an ensemble. As a class, the students should have a repertoire of at least four ensemble selections that they can play accurately and musically
18. Identify and perform in time signatures $\frac{4}{4}$, $\frac{3}{4}$ and $\frac{2}{4}$
19. Perform in a variety of tempos
20. Perform with a metronome, electronic drummer, or recorded accompaniment
21. Demonstrate through performance appropriate dynamics including forte and piano
22. Sight-read a simple melodic line of 8 measures in first position, using simple meter in the keys of C major, G major and a minor containing whole, half and quarter notes and corresponding rest rhythms

NAfME Council for Guitar Education

Best Practices Outline for a Year Two Guitar Class

YEAR TWO—At the completion of year two, students will be able to:

1. Play all notes on each string through fifth position
2. Read and play with standard notation for pitch, rhythm, meter, articulation, dynamics, and other elements of music as outlined in year one
3. Demonstrate through performance appropriate dynamics to include mezzo forte and mezzo piano
4. Read and perform rhythms and rhythmic patterns with note values including whole notes, half notes, eighth notes, sixteenth notes, eighth-note triplets, dotted halves, dotted quarters, dotted eighths and corresponding rests
5. Sight-read a moderate level melodic line of 16 measures in simple meter in the keys of C major, G major, D major, F major and a minor, b minor, e minor, and d minor containing whole, half, dotted half, quarter, dotted quarter, and eighth note, rhythms and corresponding rests in first through fifth positions
6. Play in time signatures $\frac{6}{8}$, $\frac{9}{8}$ and alla breve (cut time)
7. Play in Fifth Position in the keys of C major, a minor, F major and d minor
8. Play melodic lines in the keys of C major, a minor, D major, b minor, F major, d minor, G major, e minor, A major, f♯ minor, B♭ and g minor (three sharps and two flats)
9. Play major scales in the keys C, D, F, B♭, G, A & E and natural, and harmonic minor scales a, d, e, and b in two octaves
10. Play one form of the movable, two-octave pentatonic scale
11. Play chromatic scale in first position ascending and descending

12. Play from E3 – C6, low open e string to 8th fret of high e string
13. Play moveable barre chords based on the "E" and "A" chord forms
14. Play I–IV–V7–I in every key using moveable forms
15. Play power chords with roots on the E and A strings
16. Play major, minor, major sevenths, dominant sevenths, minor sevenths and power chords in every key using moveable forms
17. Play a standard 12-bar blues progression in a variety of keys and rhythmic styles
18. Read chord diagrams and play from lead sheets using chord symbols and diagrams
19. Strum syncopated rhythms demonstrating facilities in both pick and finger-style techniques
20. Demonstrate the ability to perform right-hand arpeggios (p-i-m-a and its variations), and alternation techniques including using a pick (Alternate picking and Travis picking)
21. Create simple melodies in ABA form
22. Participate in performance and evaluation of music
23. Become aware of musical styles and composers and their correlation to world history
24. Define and apply music terminology found in the music literature being studied
25. Perform solo guitar literature with two contrapuntal voices
26. Tune the guitar using harmonics
27. Utilize tone color changes in performance to include tasto (neck), ponticello (bridge), and pizzicato (palm muting)

Best Practices Outline for a Year Three Guitar Class

YEAR THREE—At the completion of year three, students will be able to:

1. Play all notes on each string through ninth position
2. Play "swing" eighth notes in the jazz style
3. Play in duple, triple and compound meters to include $\frac{9}{8}$, $\frac{12}{8}$
4. Recognize and interpret general articulations such as staccato, legato, tenuto, marcato, accent marks
5. Using moveable shapes, play major, natural minor, harmonic minor and melodic minor scales in every key in two octaves
6. Perform melodies in keys of **Bb major, Eb major, g minor** and **c minor**
7. Recognize and interpret ornamentations such as slides, slurs (hammer-on and pull-off), trills and mordents
8. Play two notes simultaneously using intervals of thirds, sixths and octaves
9. Play augmented and diminished chords in every key using moveable shapes and barre chords
10. Play major sixth, minor sixth, ninth, thirteenth and suspended 2nd and 4th chords using moveable shapes
11. Play intermediate-level syncopated strums
12. Perform intermediate arpeggiated studies demonstrating facilities in both flat picking (Alternate picking, Travis picking) and finger-style techniques (rest stroke—apoyano/free stroke—tirando)
13. Perform in a variety of ensemble settings

14. Evaluate career opportunities related to music and guitar
15. Perform intermediate level solo guitar literature with three to four voices
16. Demonstrate through performance appropriate dynamics including fortissimo, pianissimo, crescendo and decrescendo
17. Sight-read a moderate level melodic line of 24 measures in simple and compound meters in C major, G major, D major, A major, F major and a minor, b minor, e minor, f♯ minor, and d minor containing whole, half/dotted half, quarter/dotted quarter, and eighth note, rhythms and corresponding rests in first through seventh positions
18. Perform natural harmonics using the 5th, 7th and 12th frets

NAfME Council for Guitar Education

Best Practices Outline for a Year Four Guitar Class

YEAR FOUR—At the completion of year four, students will be able to:

1. Play the full range of the fingerboard
2. Play scordatura (alternate) tunings
3. Play Greek modes (ex. Dorian, Lydian, Mixolydian, etc.) in every key using moveable shapes in two octaves
4. Improvise over basic 12-bar blues and ii–V^7–I chord progressions in a variety of keys and rhythmic styles
5. Perform complex rhythms and syncopations
6. Perform compound duple, triple and asymmetric meters
7. Perform stylistically appropriate accompaniment techniques (ex. Latin, flamenco, rasgueado, jazz comping, palm muting)
8. Perform in a variety of small and large ensembles incorporating different styles
9. Play appropriate selected studies, ex. Carcassi, Giuliani, Sor, Leo Brouwer, William Leavitt—Modern Method for Guitar—Berklee
10. Create a chord melody arrangement from a given melody and chord symbols
11. Demonstrate advanced facilities in both flat picking and finger-style techniques, including but not limited to Sweep picking and Tremolo picking
12. Perform melodic lines in the major keys up to four sharps and four flats including relative minor keys
13. Perform advanced-level solo guitar literature with three to four voices
14. Perform artificial and pinch harmonics
15. Develop a personal portfolio for post-secondary opportunities related to music and guitar
16. Have a basic level of knowledge and skill using technology related to composition and performance (amplifiers, computers, recording software, MIDI, effects units and guitars)

Guitar Ensemble Repertoire by Bill Swick Available at J.W. Pepper

Title	Composer	Year & Quarter	Product SKU
Winds in the Morning	Traditional	Year 1 Quarter 3	BSY1Q3-30ET
Toil and Trouble	Traditional	Year 1 Quarter 3	BSY1Q3-31ET
The Sign of Bonny Blue Bell	Folk Song	Year 1 Quarter 3	BSY1Q3-32ET
Sor Study No. 1	Fernando Sor	Year 1 Quarter 3	BSY1Q3-33ET
Song Tune	Thomas Campion	Year 1 Quarter 3	BSY1Q3-34ET
Sonata in G Major	Domenico Scarlatti	Year 1 Quarter 3	BSY1Q3-35ET
Minuet	Johann Krieger	Year 1 Quarter 3	BSY1Q3-36ET
Menuett	Robert de Visée	Year 1 Quarter 3	BSY1Q3-37ET
L'Estartit	Spanish Folk Dance	Year 1 Quarter 3	BSY1Q3-38ET
C/AmStudy No. 1	Niccolò Paganini	Year 1 Quarter 3	BSY1Q3-39ET
Boureé	G.F. Handel	Year 1 Quarter 3	BSY1Q3-40ET
A Field of Secrets	F. Henry	Year 1 Quarter 3	BSY1Q3-41ET
Kojo No Tsuki	Rentarō Taki	Year 1 Quarter 4	BSY1Q4-117ET
Minuet in E Minor	Robert de Visée	Year 1 Quarter 4	BSY1Q4-119ET
Waltz No. 8	Dionisio Aguado	Year 1 Quarter 4	BSY1Q4-42ET
Trio No. 5	Ferdinando Carulli	Year 1 Quarter 4	BSY1Q4-43ET
Study No. 16-Concerto	Matteo Carcassi	Year 1 Quarter 4	BSY1Q4-44ET
Rhondo	Jean-Philippe Rameau	Year 1 Quarter 4	BSY1Q4-45ET
La Firolera	Mexican Tradition	Year 1 Quarter 4	BSY1Q4-46ET
Kemp's Jig	Anonymous	Year 1 Quarter 4	BSY1Q4-47ET
Gavot	G.F. Handel	Year 1 Quarter 4	BSY1Q4-48ET
Anglaise	J.S. Bach	Year 1 Quarter 4	BSY1Q4-49ET
Andantino in C	Fernando Sor	Year 1 Quarter 4	BSY1Q4-50ET
Andante in B Minor	Fernando Sor	Year 1 Quarter 4	BSY1Q4-51ET
Andante in A Minor	Fernando Sor	Year 1 Quarter 4	BSY1Q4-52ET
Am Study No. 12	Niccolò Paganini	Year 1 Quarter 4	BSY1Q4-53ET
Guitar Trio Movt. 2	Johann Mattheson	Year 1 Quarter 4	BSY1Q4-54ET
A Welsh Dance	Traditional	Year 1 Quarter 4	BSY1Q4-55ET
El Vito	Spanish Traditional	Year 2 Quarter 1	BSY2Q1-105MIX
Vals Venezolano No. 2	Antonio Lauro	Year 2 Quarter 1	BSY2Q1-106MIX
German Dance	W.A. Mozart	Year 2 Quarter 1	BSY2Q1-124ET
Duet Book One	Various	Year 2 Quarter 1	BSY2Q1-200ED
Magic Flute	W.A. Mozart	Year 2 Quarter 1	BSY2Q1-204EQ
Alleluia	William Boyce	Year 2 Quarter 1	BSY2Q1-56ET
Argentine Tango	Julio César Sander	Year 2 Quarter 1	BSY2Q1-57ET
Trio No. 7	Ferdinando Carulli	Year 2 Quarter 1	BSY2Q1-58ET

Title	Composer	Year & Quarter	Product SKU
Trio Op. 26 Movt IV-Rondo	Leonhard von Call	Year 2 Quarter 1	BSY2Q1-59ET
Op. 43, No. 1	Fernando Sor	Year 2 Quarter 1	BSY2Q1-60ET
Op.31, No. 23	Fernando Sor	Year 2 Quarter 1	BSY2Q1-61ET
Largo	Antonio Vivaldi	Year 2 Quarter 1	BSY2Q1-63ET
Gigue	Robert de Visée	Year 2 Quarter 1	BSY2Q1-64ET
Boureé in C	Robert de Visée	Year 2 Quarter 1	BSY2Q1-65ET
Andantino in G	Fernando Sor	Year 2 Quarter 1	BSY2Q1-66ET
Trio Op. 26 Movt I - Andante	Leonhard von Call	Year 2 Quarter 1	BSY2Q1-67ET
Allegretto in G Major	Fernando Sor	Year 2 Quarter 1	BSY2Q1-68ET
Angels We Have Heard on High	Traditional	Year 2 Quarter 2	BSY2Q2-100MIX
The Holly and the Ivy	Traditional	Year 2 Quarter 2	BSY2Q2-101MIX
Here We Come A-Wassailing	Traditional	Year 2 Quarter 2	BSY2Q2-102MIX
Up on the Housetop	Benjamin Hanby	Year 2 Quarter 2	BSY2Q2-103MIX
Angels from the Realms of Glory	H. T. Smart/James Montgomery	Year 2 Quarter 2	BSY2Q2-104MIX
Waltz in A Major-Simplified	Francisco Tárrega	Year 2 Quarter 2	BSY2Q2-118ET
Marionas	Gasper Sanz	Year 2 Quarter 2	BSY2Q2-139EQ
Passacalles in A Minor	Gasper Sanz	Year 2 Quarter 2	BSY2Q2-145EQ
Away in a Manger	Traditional	Year 2 Quarter 2	BSY2Q2-180EQ
O Come All Ye Faithful	Traditional	Year 2 Quarter 2	BSY2Q2-182EQ
Deck the Halls	Traditional	Year 2 Quarter 2	BSY2Q2-183EQ
Ding Dong Merrily on High	Jehan Tabourot	Year 2 Quarter 2	BSY2Q2-184EQ
God Rest You Merry, Gentlemen	Traditional	Year 2 Quarter 2	BSY2Q2-185EQ
Good King Wenceslas	Traditional	Year 2 Quarter 2	BSY2Q2-186EQ
Hark! The Herald Angels Sing	Felix Mendelssohn	Year 2 Quarter 2	BSY2Q2-187EQ
Joy to the World	Isaac Watts	Year 2 Quarter 2	BSY2Q2-190EQ
It Came Upon the Midnight Clear	Edmund Sears	Year 2 Quarter 2	BSY2Q2-191EQ
Silent Night	Franz Xaver Gruber	Year 2 Quarter 2	BSY2Q2-193EQ
The First Noel	Traditional	Year 2 Quarter 2	BSY2Q2-194EQ
O Little Town of Bethlehem	Traditional	Year 2 Quarter 2	BSY2Q2-196EQ
What Child is This?	William Chatterton Dix	Year 2 Quarter 2	BSY2Q2-199EQ
Trio No. 10	Ferdinando Carulli	Year 2 Quarter 2	BSY2Q2-69ET
Suite in D Minor	Robert de Visée	Year 2 Quarter 2	BSY2Q2-70ET
Study No. 8	Fernando Sor	Year 2 Quarter 2	BSY2Q2-71ET
Revolutionary Tea	Folk Song	Year 2 Quarter 2	BSY2Q2-72ET
Rigaudon	Jean-Philippe Rameau	Year 2 Quarter 2	BSY2Q2-73ET
Polonaise	Anna M. Bach	Year 2 Quarter 2	BSY2Q2-74ET

Title	Composer	Year & Quarter	Product SKU
Nine of Us Have Left	East Asian Traditional	Year 2 Quarter 2	BSY2Q2-75ET
Calypso	Jamaican Folk Dance	Year 2 Quarter 2	BSY2Q2-76ET
Op. 35, No.9 Guitar Concerto	Fernando Sor	Year 2 Quarter 2	BSY2Q2-77ET
Trio Op. 26. Movement II	Leonhard von Call	Year 2 Quarter 2	BSY2Q2-78ET
Lilliburlero	Henry Purcell	Year 2 Quarter 2	BSY2Q2-79ET
La Cucaracha	Traditional	Year 2 Quarter 2	BSY2Q2-80ET
Guitar Trio Movt. 1	Johann Mattheson	Year 2 Quarter 2	BSY2Q2-81ET
Dream Tango	E.V. Malderen	Year 2 Quarter 2	BSY2Q2-82ET
Country Dance No. 8, Op. 11	Dionisio Aguado	Year 2 Quarter 2	BSY2Q2-83ET
Canzona	Henry Purcell	Year 2 Quarter 2	BSY2Q2-84ET
Allemande	Robert de Visée	Year 2 Quarter 2	BSY2Q2-85ET
Air in E Minor	Henry Purcell	Year 2 Quarter 2	BSY2Q2-86ET
Trio Op. 26. Movement III	Leonhard von Call	Year 2 Quarter 2	BSY2Q2-87ET
Taconeado/Mexican Hat Dance	Traditional	Year 2 Quarter 3	BSY2Q3-119ET
Easy Piece No. 1	Dionisio Aguado	Year 2 Quarter 3	BSY2Q3-120ET
Easy Piece No. 3	Dionisio Aguado	Year 2 Quarter 3	BSY2Q3-121ET
Duet No. 7	Ferdinando Carulli	Year 2 Quarter 3	BSY2Q3-201ED
Still I Love Thee-Quartet	Justin Holland	Year 2 Quarter 3	BSY2Q3-203EQ
Two Guitars	Traditional	Year 2 Quarter 3	BSY2Q3-88ET
Nun Danket	Johann Crügar	Year 2 Quarter 3	BSY2Q3-89ET
Gavotte	François Couperin	Year 2 Quarter 3	BSY2Q3-90ET
Dark Eyes	Traditional	Year 2 Quarter 3	BSY2Q3-91ET
Country Dance No. 7, Op. 11	Dionisio Aguado	Year 2 Quarter 3	BSY2Q3-92ET
Country Dance No. 1, Op. 8	Dionisio Aguado	Year 2 Quarter 4	BSY2Q4-100ET
The Diamond Ring	Ferdinando Carulli	Year 2 Quarter 4	BSY2Q4-149EQ
The Rose	Ferdinando Carulli	Year 2 Quarter 4	BSY2Q4-150EQ
The Angel, Op. 333	Ferdinando Carulli	Year 2 Quarter 4	BSY2Q4-152EQ
Courant	Robert de Visée	Year 2 Quarter 4	BSY2Q4-156EQ
Trio No. 6	Ferdinando Carulli	Year 2 Quarter 4	BSY2Q4-93ET
Two Waltzes	Johann Strauss	Year 2 Quarter 4	BSY2Q4-94ET
Vals Sereno	Traditional	Year 2 Quarter 4	BSY2Q4-95ET
Trio No. 11	Ferdinando Carulli	Year 2 Quarter 4	BSY2Q4-96ET
Study No. 13	Fernando Sor	Year 2 Quarter 4	BSY2Q4-97ET
Packington's Pound	Traditional	Year 2 Quarter 4	BSY2Q4-98ET
La Firolera	Traditional	Year 2 Quarter 4	BSY2Q4-99ET
To a Wild Rose	Edward MacDonald	Year 3 Quarter 1	BSY3Q1-101ET
Hunter's Round	Artôt	Year 3 Quarter 1	BSY3Q1-123EQ
Funeral March	Fernando Sor	Year 3 Quarter 1	BSY3Q1-126EQ
Gigue	François Couperin	Year 3 Quarter 1	BSY3Q1-131EQ
Concerto alla Rustica Op. 52. No. 4	Antonio Vivaldi	Year 3 Quarter 1	BSY3Q1-132EQ
Celtic Jig	Traditional Irish Folk Song	Year 3 Quarter 1	BSY3Q1-136EQ
Fuga	Gasper Sanz	Year 3 Quarter 1	BSY3Q1-143EQ

Title	Composer	Year & Quarter	Product SKU
Villanos	Gasper Sanz	Year 3 Quarter 1	BSY3Q1-144EQ
Fuga No. 2 in D Minor	Gasper Sanz	Year 3 Quarter 1	BSY3Q1-146EQ
The Pasture, Op. 333	Ferdinando Carulli	Year 3 Quarter 1	BSY3Q1-147EQ
Haydn Theme Movts 1 & 2	Johannes Brahms	Year 3 Quarter 1	BSY3Q1-154EQ
Caprice No. 14	Niccolò Paganini	Year 3 Quarter 1	BSY3Q1-155EQ
Sonata No. 11	Franz Joseph Haydn	Year 3 Quarter 1	BSY3Q1-159EQ
When Irish Eyes are Smiling	Traditional Irish Folk Song	Year 3 Quarter 1	BSY3Q1-173EQ
Grand Quartet Salon	Johann Wenzel Kalliwoda	Year 3 Quarter 1	BSY3Q1-201EQ
Table Music for Two Guitars	W.A. Mozart	Year 3 Quarter 1	BSY3Q1-211ED
La Prima Donna Waltz	Justin Holland	Year 3 Quarter 1	BSY3Q1-213ED
Keppel's Delight	Folk Song	Year 3 Quarter 2	BSY3Q2-103ET
Gavotte	Alessandro Scarlatti	Year 3 Quarter 2	BSY3Q2-104ET
Spanish Dance No. 2	Enrique Granados	Year 3 Quarter 2	BSY3Q2-105ET
Paddy Whack	Folk Song	Year 3 Quarter 2	BSY3Q2-106ET
March in F Major	Fernando Sor	Year 3 Quarter 2	BSY3Q2-107ET
Largo-Allegro	Henry Purcell	Year 3 Quarter 2	BSY3Q2-108ET
Vals Op 8, No. 4	Agustín Barrios Mangore	Year 3 Quarter 2	BSY3Q2-122ET
The Maiden	Ferdinando Carulli	Year 3 Quarter 2	BSY3Q2-148EQ
Presto	John Helmich Roman	Year 3 Quarter 2	BSY3Q2-162EQ
Wondering Willie	Scottish Folk Song	Year 3 Quarter 2	BSY3Q2-174EQ
Zarabanda	Enrique Granados	Year 3 Quarter 2	BSY3Q2-175EQ
Angels from the Realms of Glory	James Montgomery	Year 3 Quarter 2	BSY3Q2-178EQ
Angels we Have Heard on High	Traditional	Year 3 Quarter 2	BSY3Q2-179EQ
Hebrew Medley	Traditional	Year 3 Quarter 2	BSY3Q2-188EQ
Up on the Housetop	Benjamin Hanby	Year 3 Quarter 2	BSY3Q2-197EQ
We Wish You a Merry Christmas	Traditional	Year 3 Quarter 2	BSY3Q2-198EQ
Theme from Op. 102	Mauro Giuliani	Year 3 Quarter 3	BSY3Q3-109ET
Study No. 12	Fernando Sor	Year 3 Quarter 3	BSY3Q3-110ET
Menuett in F Major	Fernando Sor	Year 3 Quarter 3	BSY3Q3-111ET
El Vito	Spanish Traditional	Year 3 Quarter 3	BSY3Q3-112ET
Easy Piece No. 2	Dionisio Aguado	Year 3 Quarter 3	BSY3Q3-113ET
Quartet Op. 21. Movt. 1	Ferdinando Carulli	Year 3 Quarter 3	BSY3Q3-119EQ
Quartet No. 6 in C Major Op.1, No. 6	Joseph Haydn	Year 3 Quarter 3	BSY3Q3-120EQ
Arada	F. Moreno Torroba	Year 3 Quarter 3	BSY3Q3-138EQ
Maricapalos	Gasper Sanz	Year 3 Quarter 3	BSY3Q3-140EQ
Espanoletas	Gasper Sanz	Year 3 Quarter 3	BSY3Q3-142EQ
The Soft Breeze	Ferdinando Carulli	Year 3 Quarter 3	BSY3Q3-151EQ
Eine Kleine Nachtmusic	W.A. Mozart	Year 3 Quarter 3	BSY3Q3-157EQ
Vals Venezolano No 2	Antonio Lauro	Year 3 Quarter 3	BSY3Q3-170EQ
Zambra Granadina	Isaac Albéniz	Year 3 Quarter 3	BSY3Q3-200EQ
Duet No. 9	Ferdinando Carulli	Year 3 Quarter 3	BSY3Q3-202ED

Title	Composer	Year & Quarter	Product SKU
Duet No. 10	Ferdinando Carulli	Year 3 Quarter 3	BSY3Q3-203ED
Canon in D	Johann Pachelbel	Year 3 Quarter 3	BSY3Q3-204ED
Sonata L. 483	Domenico Scarlatti	Year 3 Quarter 3	BSY3Q3-208ED
Swinging in the Key of Bb Major	Jazz Standard	Year 3 Quarter 3	BSY3Q3-302EQ
Bebop Boogie in F Major	Jazz Standard	Year 3 Quarter 3	BSY3Q3-303EQ
Bebop in G	Jazz Standard	Year 3 Quarter 3	BSY3Q3-304EQ
Study No. 20	Fernando Sor	Year 3 Quarter 4	BSY3Q4-114ET
Study No. 18	Fernando Sor	Year 3 Quarter 4	BSY3Q4-115ET
Scarlatti Sonata	Domenico Scarlatti	Year 3 Quarter 4	BSY3Q4-116ET
Dance of the Goblins	Antonio Bazzini	Year 3 Quarter 4	BSY3Q4-130EQ
Canarios	Gasper Sanz	Year 3 Quarter 4	BSY3Q4-141EQ
Vals Venezolano No 3	Antonio Lauro	Year 3 Quarter 4	BSY3Q4-171EQ
Allegro 12 Concerti Op 6	G.F. Handel	Year 3 Quarter 4	BSY3Q4-176EQ
Cuckoo's Nest	Folk Song	Year 3 Quarter 4	BSY3Q4-177EQ
Sonata L. 263	Domenico Scarlatti	Year 3 Quarter 4	BSY3Q4-206ED
Minor Bebop	Jazz Standard	Year 3 Quarter 4	BSY3Q4-301EQ
Suite No. 4 in E Minor	G.F. Handel	Year 4 Quarter 1	BSY4Q1-123EQ
Fugue in E Minor	J.S. Bach	Year 4 Quarter 1	BSY4Q1-127EQ
Diabelli No. 1	Anton Diabelli	Year 4 Quarter 1	BSY4Q1-128EQ
Choros No. 1	Heitor Villa-Lobos	Year 4 Quarter 1	BSY4Q1-133EQ
Chason	Manual Ponce	Year 4 Quarter 1	BSY4Q1-134EQ
Chaconne in F Major	G.F. Handel	Year 4 Quarter 1	BSY4Q1-135EQ
The Cat's Fugue k.30	Domenico Scarlatti	Year 4 Quarter 1	BSY4Q1-137EQ
Danza Brasilera	Jorge Morel	Year 4 Quarter 1	BSY4Q1-153EQ
Symphonie de Haydn Op 152	Ferdinando Carulli	Year 4 Quarter 1	BSY4Q1-168EQ
Tu Y Yo Gavota	Agustín Barrios Mangore	Year 4 Quarter 1	BSY4Q1-169EQ
Still I Love Thee-Duet	Justin Holland	Year4 Quarter 1	BSY4Q1-214ED
El Rossinyol	Traditional Catalan	Year 4 Quarter 2	BSY4Q2-117ET
Rondo	Ferdinando Carulli	Year 4 Quarter 2	BSY4Q2-163EQ
Symphony No 40 in G Minor k550	W.A. Mozart	Year 4 Quarter 2	BSY4Q2-167EQ
Christmas Medley	Traditional	Year 4 Quarter 2	BSY4Q2-181EQ
Here We Come A-Wassailing	Traditional	Year 4 Quarter 2	BSY4Q2-189EQ
Nutcracker Jingles	Traditional	Year 4 Quarter 2	BSY4Q2-192EQ
The Holly and the Ivy	Traditional	Year 4 Quarter 2	BSY4Q2-195EQ
La Fille Du Regiment-Donizetti	Justin Holland	Year 4, Quarter 2	BSY4Q2-202EQ
Rondo	Ferdinando Carulli	Year 4 Quarter 2	BSY4Q2-205ED
Sonata L. 395	Domenico Scarlatti	Year 4 Quarter 2	BSY4Q2-207ED
Sonata	Domenico Scarlatti	Year 4 Quarter 2	BSY4Q2-209ED
La Fille Du Regiment-Donizetti-Duet	Justin Holland	Year 4 Quarter 2	BSY4Q2-212ED
Quartet No. 6	François de Fossa	Year 4 Quarter 3	BSY4Q3-121EQ
La Banatina	Agustín Barrios Mangore	Year 4 Quarter 3	BSY4Q3-122EQ

Title	Composer	Year & Quarter	Product SKU
Grand Solo	Fernando Sor	Year 4 Quarter 3	BSY4Q3-124EQ
Granada	Isaac Albéniz	Year 4 Quarter 3	BSY4Q3-125EQ
Homage to Tarrega	Joaquín Turina	Year 4 Quarter 3	BSY4Q3-160EQ
New Serenade	Ferdinando Carulli	Year 4 Quarter 3	BSY4Q3-161EQ
Sevilla Suite Espanola	Isaac Albéniz	Year 4 Quarter 3	BSY4Q3-164EQ
Symphonie de Haydn, Op. 152	Ferdinando Carulli	Year 4 Quarter 3	BSY4Q3-210ED
English Suite	John W. Duarte	Year 4 Quarter 4	BSY4Q4-118ET
Quartet 8, Movt. 2	Dmitri Shostakovich	Year 4 Quarter 4	BSY4Q4-165EQ
Sonatina Movements 1-3	F. Moreno Torroba	Year 4 Quarter 4	BSY4Q4-166EQ

APPENDIX D

Consent Form

Each school district will have its own form for faculty to distribute and collect in order to comply with COPPA, the Children's Online Privacy Protection Act. Here are three examples of forms used by the Clark County School District.

9998-500562   CCF-562
                                                                                                          4/06

Clark County School District
MEDIA RELEASE FORM

Dear Parent/Guardian:

At times during and after the school day, school personnel and/or news media may ask to interview, photograph, audiotape, film and/or videotape students. This material may be utilized in media that includes, but is not limited to, the following: newspaper articles, television coverage, websites, internal or external publications, newsletters, video presentations, and/or school district presentations.

Your signature on the form below authorizes the school and/or school district to release your child's name, photograph, and/or audio/video/film production for publication related to school functions and activities. Examples may include, but are not limited to, student activities, individual or group achievements, sporting events, musical or theatrical presentations, and/or discussion forums.

Once signed and dated, this form shall remain in effect until the end of the current school year. At any time during the school year, however, you may revoke this permission for future use by notifying, in writing, the principal of your child's school.

_____

As the parent/guardian of _____ , I

Student Name (please print)

_____ Give permission

_____ Do not give permission

for the Clark County School District to release my child's name, photograph, and/or audio/video/film reproduction for publication, broadcast or posting to the CCSD.net website, as described above.

_____
Printed Name of Parent/Guardian

_____ _____
Signature of Parent/Guardian   Date

012/100

CLARK COUNTY SCHOOL DISTRICT RELEASE FORM AND WAIVER
For Students and Employees

This Is a Legal Document Affecting Your Rights and Responsibilities
Please Read it Carefully Before Signing

1.   I understand that _____ ("Producer") and _____
("Company") is producing a currently untitled documentary film concerning
_____ (the "Picture" or "Program"), and has contacted me for
participation. Producer is interested in obtaining film, video or other footage including
audio ("Footage") through interviews and related activities.

2.   I understand that my participation is entirely voluntary and that making the Picture
will occur completely apart from my obligations as a student and/or outside the course
and scope of my job duties as an employee. I also understand that I am not being
directed or otherwise compelled by the Clark County School District ("District") to
participate in the making of the Picture. I understand that no grade or performance
evaluation may be based on my decision to participate or abstain from participation in
making this Picture.

3.   I understand that filming is to occur on the property of the District, namely
_____ School, and that my comments, actions, or image may be
associated with the District and that I have a duty to maintain a professional decorum
when making any statements that are made on behalf of the District, or any statements
that may be construed as those of the District because of the nature of the subject matter
or the environment in which the statements were provided.

4.   As a District employee (if applicable), I understand that I am obligated to protect
the privacy and confidential information of students and that I may not share that
information without the consent of the legal guardian, parent or student, whichever is
appropriate.

5.   I understand that the Producer or its affiliates may use all or part of any Footage
including sections that have been edited or spliced together and portions that did not
occur in chronological or sequential order in the production of the Picture.

6.   I understand that the District has no control over the Producer's decisions
regarding the Picture and therefore the District has no responsibility or liability to me, my
reputation or anyone associated with me as it relates to the making of this Picture or the
end result of this Picture. I understand that I may disagree with the final edited version of
the Picture and may feel that it is disparaging or defamatory.

7.   I understand that the Picture may be shown in any market, including
internationally, and may be repeated in part or as a whole, indefinitely. I understand that
my words or actions may be taken out of context. I further understand that the Picture

CLARK COUNTY SCHOOL DISTRICT RELEASE FORM AND WAIVER
For Students and Employees

may be aired on television, video, movies or other methods of production and that the end result may call into question my words, actions, character, personal ethics or professional integrity.

8.   I understand I am waiving my rights to sue or otherwise pursue any legal remedy against the District for any action or omission, intentional or accidental that may arise from the making of the final product or the Picture.

9.   I understand that the District will not be obligated to defend or indemnify me should a dispute arise against me in relation to this Picture. I also understand that the District will not initiate or maintain any litigation on my behalf in connection with the Picture.

10.   I understand that this release and waiver may be in addition to the same type of document presented to me by the Producer, but is required prior to any filming or other media activities in which I may appear. This waiver and release is for the clarification and protection of the District.

If releaser is 18 years old or older, complete the following:

Print Name: _____

Signature: _____

Date: _____

If releaser is not yet 18 years old, complete the following:

I, the undersigned, hereby warrant that I am the Parent/Guardian of _____, a minor, and have full authority to authorize the above release and waiver which I have read an approved.

Print Name of Parent/Guardian: _____

Signature: _____

On Behalf of _____ (minor's name)

Date: _____

VENUE RELEASE BETWEEN
_____ AND
CLARK COUNTY SCHOOL DISTRICT

LOCATION: _____ School, located at _____,
Las Vegas, Nevada _____ **DATE:** _____

Brief description of the filming/project: _____
_____
_____

1. General Terms

This grant and release (this **"Release"**) is entered into effective as of the date set forth
below. Clark County School District (**"CCSD"**) hereby grants to _____
(**"Producer"**), and any person or entity authorized by Producer permission to:

(a) Photograph and record at the CCSD property named _____ School,
located at _____, Las Vegas, Nevada (**"Location"**; or **"Venue"**
when referenced together with CCSD) in mutually agreed upon locations therein
(on film, videotape, audiotape, digital media or otherwise),

(b) Edit and modify any resulting photographs, recordings or other media or
materials (the **"Photographs and Recordings"**) subject to Sections 6, 7, and 8
of this Release, and

(c) Use and distribute the Photographs and Recordings subject to Sections 6, 7,
and 8 of this Release.

2. Property Rights Regarding Photographs and Recordings

CCSD further understands and agrees that Producer will own all rights of any kind in the
Photographs and Recordings, and that CCSD will retain no rights therein. CCSD further
understands that Producer shall have no obligation to make any use of the Photographs
or Recordings and that all rights granted in this Release are fully sublicensable and
assignable. However, CCSD requires review, approval, and release of photographs,
recordings or other media produced on their property. At no time will CCSD permit a
negative portrayal of a school, CCSD, or affiliated persons being recorded or
photographed. This process in no way relieves Producer of the responsibility to obtain
all necessary releases and approvals of any parties that may be involved in the media
use indicated herein.

3. Consideration

CCSD hereby acknowledges that Producer has separately paid consideration (the **"Consideration"**) to CCSD for the right to use the Location. CCSD hereby acknowledges and agrees that the Consideration shall be the only consideration and payment required to be transferred by Producer or its affiliates to CCSD in exchange for the permission granted, and agreements set forth, in this Release. For the avoidance of doubt, CCSD acknowledges and agrees that CCSD shall not be entitled to receive any additional compensation for any use by Producer or its affiliates or designees of any of the Photographs and Recordings.

4. Approval of the Principal and Assistant Chief Student Achievement Officer

The date(s) and time(s) of the above described permissions to enter, occupy, and/or use the Location have been approved by the Principal and the Assistant Chief Student Achievement Officer of _____ School.

5. Applicable Licenses or Permits Required by City, County, or State

Producer is responsible to obtain and maintain any required permits or permissions required by city, county, or state officials.

6. Endorsement

Producer agrees that the Photographs and Recordings will not imply any endorsement of Producer by CCSD, and should include the following disclaimer: *"The Clark County School District does not endorse this commercial company or its products."*

7. Use of Logos

Producer must obtain final approval of any use of the Venue's name, logo, signs, marks or slogans used in the Photographs and Recordings. Producer shall not edit or modify the Photographs and Recordings in a manner that is derogatory, defamatory, slanderous, censorable, or untrue with respect to the Venue, CCSD, or its employees or students.

8. Remove Proprietary or Personal Information

Producer has been advised that various materials and displays at the Location may contain proprietary or personally identifiable information of individuals or companies. It is the responsibility of Producer to temporarily remove/sanitize the information or to obtain the necessary clearance/release to include the information in the Photographs and Recordings.

9. Ability to Stop Filming

Should CCSD find in its reasonable discretion that any activities being conducted are detrimental to the Venue, illegal in any manner, or dangerous in nature, CCSD shall have the authority to temporarily halt activities until concerns are resolved, or to otherwise require resolution of the problem.

10. Safety Precautions and Programs

Producer shall be solely responsible for initiating, maintaining and supervising all safety precautions and programs in connection with the performance of this Release.

11. Indemnity and Liability

Producer will protect, defend, indemnify and hold harmless CCSD and all CCSD's agents and employees from and against all claims, damages, losses and expenses, including attorney's fees, arising out of, attributable to, or resulting from the performance of Producer's work whether it is caused in part or in whole by a party indemnified under the Release.

Producer assumes liability and responsibility for all its activities at the Location. Producer also assumes liability and responsibility for the Photographs and Recordings and any use thereof in media now known to exist or that becomes known in the future.

12. Insurance Requirements

Producer shall provide evidence of the following insurance coverages.

(a) Commercial General Liability in an amount not less than $1 million each occurrence, naming (and providing endorsement for) Clark County School District as an additional insured.

(b) Errors and Omissions coverage in an amount not less than $1 million, naming Clark County School District as a named insured for this production.

(c) Statutory Worker's Compensation/Employer's Liability insurance in an amount not less than $1 million, also providing a waiver of subrogation in favor of the Clark County School District.

13. Non-Assignability

Neither Producer nor CCSD may assign any part or all of this Release without the consent of the other party.

14. Third Party Disclaimer

This Release is made for the benefit of the parties to the Release, and not for any outside party.

15. Authority to Execute and Release

Both parties assert that they have all necessary powers and authority to execute and deliver this Release. The execution, delivery and performance of this Release has been duly and validly authorized by all necessary corporate, limited liability company or other similar entity action.

16. Agreement to Terms

Both parties hereby attest that they have read and agree to the terms of this Release.

17. Release is Irrevocable

This Release is irrevocable, so that Producer may proceed in reliance thereon.

ACKNOWLEDGED AND AGREED:

Name: Clark County School District
Title: Assistant Chief Student Achievement Officer
Signature: _____
Print Name: _____
Address: _____
                  _____
Phone: _____
Email(optional): _____

ACKNOWLEDGED AND AGREED:

Producer Name: _____
Signature: _____
Print Name: _____
Title: _____
Address: _____
                  _____
Phone: _____
Email(optional): _____

Sample Program

LAS VEGAS ACADEMY

FALL
GUITAR
CONCERT

"Playing the Classics"
Featuring:
Varsity 2 & 3 Guitar Ensembles

Friday, October 4, 2019
7:00 p.m.
Lowden Theater

Guitar Concert

Varsity 2 Guitar Ensemble

Chason-Manual Ponce

Dulcinea-Mark Anthony Cruz

Manzanares Del Real-Federico Moreno Torroba

Rio De Janeiro Suite I. Maxixe-Jurg Kindle

Milongon-Argentina-Vito Nicola Paradiso

Muneira from Suite Compostelana-Frederico Mompou

Poisoned Apple-Jurg Kindle

Varsity 3 Guitar Ensemble

Hommage to Tarrega-Joaquin Turina

I. Garrotin

II. Soleares

Granda "Suite Espanola"-Isaac Albeniz

Cordoba-Isaac Albeniz

Cairo-Brent Robitaille

Air-Shingo Fujii

Quartet VI for Guitar-Francois de Fossa

Chaconne in F Major-George Frederick Handel

Rondeau de Mozart-Ferdinando Carulli

VARSITY 2 GUITAR ENSEMBLE
(last names of students were removed)

Abigail	Evan	Kaitlyn
Aziel	Bradley	Lauren
Kyle	Abel	Kylie
Jaden	Isaac	Ethyn
Jonah	Muratagic	William
Miles	Dominick	Tamia
Matthew	Shauna	Gabriel
Joycie		

VARSITY 3 GUITAR ENSEMBLE

Deven	**Sergio**	Erik
Aiste	Josue	Sophia
Taizja	Paola	Kevin
Jaelynn	**Anthony**	Emma
Dean	Coby	**Kirun**
Noah	**Jayden**	**Paolo**
Dayna	**Anthony**	Iris
Raiden	John	Aiden
Karen	**Seth**	**Alexandria**
Samuel	Hannah	

Bill Swick-Director

Names appearing in bold print represent seniors.

Andrew York to Appear at the Las Vegas Academy

World renowned, GRAMMY-award winning guitarist and composer Andrew York will appear at the Las Vegas Academy of the Arts on Friday, November 1 at 7:00 p.m. in the Performing Arts Center. Mr. York's appearance is a part of the Clark County School District High School and Middle School Honor Guitar Ensembles' weekend of activities. The public school honor guitar ensembles will perform in the same location on Saturday, November 2 at 7:00 p.m.

This is a rare opportunity for CCSD guitar students to attend a performance by such a noted guitarist. Many high school guitar students currently perform compositions by Andrew York, have watched his videos and have purchased his recordings. An opportunity to see Mr. York perform live is an amazing opportunity. In order to make this opportunity affordable, all tickets for Andrew York's performance are only $10.00. This concert is open to the community. Tickets are available online at www.LasVegasAcademy.net. Tickets are being sold as reserved seating, so purchase tickets early to assure the best seats.

In Mr. York's concerts, the theater becomes a living room, and the musical conversation begins with the first note. His authenticity has inspired a worldwide following, with his touring schedule spanning more than thirty countries. This will be a musical evening to remember.

LVA Administration
Scott Walker—Principal
Joshua Hager-Assistant Principal
Jennifer Shuler—Assistant Principal
Susan Thornton—Assistant Principal
Sarah Robinson—Dean

Joel Diamond—Counselor
Carol Dunlap—Counselor
Katherine Hackbart—Counselor
Rashida Jeffrey—Counselor
Salima Virani—Counselor

Theater Managers
Aleks Wade-Lowden Theater
Kelly Dorn-Performing Arts Center

Music Faculty
Patrick Bowen-Jazz, Percussion
Tony Branco-Piano, Music Technology
Katie Canfield-Piano, Hand Bells
Rossana Cota-Choir
Brian Downey-Band, Philharmonic
Megan Franke-Choir, Opera, Vocal Jazz
Eric McAllister-Orchestra, Philharmonic
Cecil Myers-Music Theory, Jazz Band
David Rivera-Mariachi
John Seaton-Band, Muisc Theory
Lindsey Springer-Orchestra, Philharmonic
William Swick-Guitar

Music Staff
Nicki Avery-Choir Assistant
Karen Camuglia-Band Assistant
Selene Favela-Mariachi Assistance
Juliann McAllister-Orchestra Assistance
Chalice Lundquist-Choir Assistant
Sue Mirman-Jazz Band Assistant

UPCOMING EVENTS

October 18 (Friday) Guitar Recital-Black Box-2:30 p.m. & 7:00 p.m. $8.00 admission

October 28 (Monday) LVA Gala at the Rio Hotel

November 1, Friday 7:00 p.m. Andrew York-Performing Arts Center-All tickets $10.00

November 2, Saturday 7:00 p.m. CCSD Middle & High School Honor Guitar Ensembles-Performing Arts Center-Free

December 4, Wednesday-CCSD High School Honor Guitar Ensemble performs at the Smith Center at 6:30 p.m.   Tickets are $15.

December 13, Friday 7:00 p.m. "Trans Siberian Guitar Orchestra" -Performing Arts Center-Holiday Reception to follow concert-$8

Visit our website at:
www.classroomguitar.com

Become FaceBook friends with the LVA Guitar Program

"This program is presented in accordance with CCSD Policy and Regulation 6130, Assemblies and Public Programs."

Code for Level

Title:

Composer:

Arranger:

Time Signature:

Key:

Highest Note:

Most Complex Rhythm:

Tempo:

Number of Parts:

Style:

Number of Measures:

Additional Information:

Using the NAfME Guitar Education Best Practices (Appendix B), determine which year level and quarter would be appropriate for this title.

Level: Year: Quarter:

Musical Terms to Introduce during Rehearsals

accelerando	forte	rasgado
accidentals	frets	relative minor
accompaniment	gut strings	rest stroke
add 2	harmonized scale	rests
allegretto	hemiola	ritardando
allegro	intonation	root
alphabeto	introduction	rubato
andante	inversion	saddle
andantino	jury	scales
arpeggios	key tones	sharps
articulation	lines and spaces	slack key
artificial harmonic	lute	soundboard
cadence	major seventh	staccato
cantabile	marcato	strumming
chord voicings	medley	subdivide
chordophone	minor	subdominant
chromatics	modes	subito
color tones	natural harmonic	suspended
courses	nut	syncopation
da capo	octave	tasto
dal segno	ostinato	tempo
dominant	pedal tone	tessitura
down stroke	pentatonic scale	third
Dreadnought	performance	timbre
dynamics	phrasing	tonal center
eighth notes	piano	tonic
eleventh chord	pizzicato	transposition
enharmonic names	ponticello	turnaround
evaluation	power chords	up stroke
fifth	preparation	vihuela
flats	raise 2	well-tempered scale

Sample College Audition Requirements

Most university websites have audition information for each instrument. For starters, here are the current requirements to audition for guitar at the Julliard School of Music.

1. Two contrasting movements of a J. S. Bach suite, partita, or sonata (includes Prelude, Fugue, and Allegro, BWV998)
2. Two études by Heitor Villa-Lobos
3. A complete work of any period
4. Two contrasting works
   a. One Renaissance, Classical (e.g., Sor, Giuliani, Regondi, Mertz), or nineteenth century
   b. One by a twentieth-century composer of any style
5. A spoken narrative (video recording) of up to four minutes in length, discussing all of the following
   a. Your goals and aspirations as a guitarist and musician
   b. When you first began studying classical guitar, and who are your current and former teachers
   c. Your other (non-guitar) interests

Here is a less formal audition description from the University of Memphis.

Applicants whose primary instrument is Classical Guitar should prepare the following:

- Major and minor Segovia or Shearer scales, two or three octaves
- Three contrasting pieces from three different periods, memorized

Guitar applicants seeking School of Music talent-based performance scholarships must have had a minimum of three years of classical guitar private instruction in order to play a scholarship audition.

The following audition requirements from the Jacobs School of Music at Indiana University Bloomington are fairly typical of most university requirements.

Audition repertoire requirements are the following:

- J. S. Bach—*Prelude* from Cello Suite No. 1
- Fernando Sor—one study of numbers 11–20 (Segovia edition)
- Heitor Villa-Lobos—*Prelude No. 4*, or a work of similar difficulty
- *B.M. applicants only*: Heitor Villa-Lobos —*Study No. 1*, or a work of similar difficulty

Goals Within Reach

Name: Quarter: Year:
  Annual Goals
  Year   1   2   3   4 (circle one)

1. What do you really want to accomplish this year as a guitar student? To help you answer this question, complete the following exercise:
2. List five things you would like to accomplish this school year in the order of importance to you.
   a. _____
   b. _____
   c. _____
   d. _____
   e. _____
3. List five thing you are willing to do to make these goals become a reality.
   a. _____
   b. _____
   c. _____
   d. _____
   e. _____
4. Once you have completed the above exercise, make an effort to tie the two together. For example, if in line "2a" you write, "to become a better sight-reader" and in line "3a" you write, "practice harder," make a complete thought in between these two lines. For example, "I will practice harder to become a better sight-reader." Complete the following exercise by completing each of the five sentences, starting with the words "I will."
5.
   a. I will _____.
   b. I will _____.
   c. I will _____.
   d. I will _____.
   e. I will _____.
   Samples of what your goals may look like when completed:
   a. I will play the guitar with perfect hand positions.
   b. I will read music with ease and accuracy.
   c. I will practice the guitar with intent and focus.
   d. I will play the guitar with joy.
   e. I will perform in front of others with great pleasure and without fears.
Before starting this project, give the process some thought and really focus on the goals you would like to set for yourself. Be realistic! Set goals that you can accomplish in nine months. Also, set goals that can be measured in some way.
   For example, I will play the Minute Waltz in 56 seconds (that is measurable).
   Or, I will receive 90 percent or better on all playing tests (that is measurable).
   We will revisit your goals at mid-year and again at the end of the year.

Notes

Chapter 1

1. B. Swick, "Observations of Guitar Class in 50 States," *Teaching Music*: A Publication of the National Association of Music Education 28, no. 3 (2021): 44–48 https://nafme. org/observations-of-guitar-class-in-50-states.
2. R. Pethel, "The State of Guitar Education in the United States," *Journal of Popular Music Education* 3, no. 2 (2019): 245–260, https://doi.org/10.1386/jpme.3.2.245_1.
3. Alfred S. Townsend, *Introduction to Effective Music Teaching: Artistry and Attitude* (Lanham, MD: Rowman & Littlefield, 2011).
4. Olivia Gribben, "Music Teacher Qualities That Students Look for," Waverview.com, July 17, 2020, https://wavereview.com/blog/best-music-teacher.
5. Jordan Smith has been a contributor to CMUSE since February 2015. He served as editor from July 2016 until February 2017. "10 Qualities of a Great Music Teacher," CMUSE, July 1, 2018, https://www.cmuse.org/10-qualities-of-a-great-music-teacher/.
6. Jason Sagebiel, "The Top 8 Qualities to Look for in a Great Music Teacher," Sage Music, September 15, 2020, retrieved March 14, 2021, https://www.sagemusic.co/top-8-qualities-look-great-music-teacher.
7. Don Gayhardt, *7 Important Characteristics of an Excellent Music Teacher,* June 6, 2017, retrieved June 6, 2017, https://dongayhardt.weebly.com/blog/7-important- characteristics-of-an-excellent-music-teacher
8. David Andrew Wiebe, "10 Essential Characteristics of Successful Music Instructors," in *The New Music Industry: Adapting, Growing and Thriving in the Information Age,* by Shaun Letang, Music Industry How-to," July 30, 2015, retrieved December 29, 2020, https://www.musicindustryhowto.com/10-essential-characteristics-of-successful-music-instructors-and-teachers.
9. Anthony "Tony" Mazzocchi, "What Makes a Great Music Teacher?," September 29, 2015, The Music Parents' Guide, http://www.musicparentsguide.com/2015/09/29/what-makes-a-great-music-teacher.
10. Learnivore, "Qualities of a Great Music Teacher," October 14, 2015, https://learnivore. com/users/learnivoremarketing1/posts/qualities-of-a-great-music-teacher
11. "7 Essential Qualities Every Music Teacher Should Have," May 18, 2019, https://www. millioncenters.com/blog/7-essential-qualities-every-music-teacher-should-have.
12. Noa Kageyama, "19 Things That Great Music Teachers Do," The Creativity Post, March 25, 2016, retrieved March 25, 2016, https://www.creativitypost.com/article/19_things_that_great_music_teachers_do.

Chapter 2

1. John C. Maxwell, *Teamwork Makes the Dream Work* (Nashville, TN: J. Countryman, 2002).
2. Emily Ward, "Getting Parents Involved in the Music Program," Music Travel Consultants, 2021, https://www.musictravel.com/blog/2017/11/15/getting-parents-involved-in-the-music-program.
3. Jason Marshall, "Getting Parents Involved in the Music Program," Music Travel Consultants, 2021, https://www.musictravel.com/blog/2017/11/15/getting-parents-involved-in-the-music-program.
4. Ward, "Getting Parents Involved."

Chapter 6

1. Ray Dankenbring, *The Mel Bay Story* (Pacific, MO: Mel Bay Publications, 1997).
2. Jerry Snyder, letter to Bill Swick, January 2020.
3. Thomas F. Heck, Harvey Turnbull, Paul Sparks, James Tyler, Tony Bacon, Oleg V. Timofeyev, and Gerhard Kubik, "Guitar," *Grove Music Online*, https://doi.org/10.1093/gmo/9781561592630.article.06714.
4. Christoper Page, *The Guitar in Georgian England: A Social and Music History* (Cambridge: Cambridge University Press, 2020); Page, *The Guitar in Stuart England: A Social and Musical History* (Cambridge: Cambridge University Press, 2017); Page, *The Guitar in Tudor England: A Social and Musical History* (Cambridge: Cambridge University Press, 2015).
5. "Our History Is Guitar History," n.d., Augustinestrings.com, accessed March 18, 2021, https://augustinestrings.com/history.
6. "Martin History," n.d., Martinguitar.com, accessed March 18, 2021, https://www.martinguitar.com/about-martin-martin-history.html.
7. Kenneth Peres, "Will Playing Classical Guitar Make Playing Electric Guitar Easier?" *Quora*, www.quora.com/Will-playing-classical-guitar-make-playing-electric-guitar-easier.
8. Swick, "Observations of Guitar Class in 50 States."
9. Bill Swick, *Teaching Beginning Guitar Class: A Practical Guide* (New York: Oxford University Press, 2017).

Chapter 7

1. John T. Molloy, *John T Molloy's New Dress for Success* (New York: Warner Books, 1988) 1988.

Chapter 8

1. Email to James Yancey.
2. John C. Maxwell, *Teamwork Makes the Dream Work*.
3. Email to Ruth LeMay.

Chapter 9

1. Zach VanderGraaff, "10 Music Education Grants You Can Apply For," https://solfeg.io/music-education-grants.

Chapter 10

1. Email from Jayson Martinez.

Chapter 12

1. "Facts and Figures Concerning Music and Higher Education in the United States," https://www.music.org/pdf/mihe/facts.pdf.
2. Clint Page, "Top 10 Skills for High-School Students," https://familyeducation.com/school/high-school-milestones-obstacles/top-10-skills-high-school-students.
3. Email from Jayson Martinez.
4. Fuller, Richard Buckminster, *Critical Path*. St. Martin's Press, 1981.
5. Eric Schmidt and Jared Cohen, *The New Digital Age: Reshaping the Future of People, Nations and Business* (Murray, 2014) (New York: Knopf Doubleday Publishing Group, 2013).
6. Rohn, Jim. "Commitment Quotes from Highly Successful People." *Commitment Quotes from Highly Successful People*, https://www.masteringmotivation.com/commitment-quotes.html.
7. Sara B. Johnson, Robert W. Blum, and Jay N. Giedd, "Adolescent Maturity and the Brain: The Promise and Pitfalls of Neuroscience Research in Adolescent Health Policy," *Journal of Adolescent Health: Official Publication of the Society for Adolescent Medicine* (September 2009), www.ncbi.nlm.nih.gov/pmc/articles/PMC2892678/.
8. Lolly Daskal, *The Leadership Gap: What Gets between You and Your Greatness* (New York: Portfolio/Penguin, 2017).
9. Elisa Jones, "7 Things They Don't Teach Music Education Majors (That You'll Wish They Had)," NAMfE, http://nafme.org/7-things-dont-teach-music-education-majors-youll-wish.

Appendix B

1. The text of this can also be found online at NAfME.org: https://nafme.org/wp-content/uploads/2019/05/NAfME-Guitar-Council-Best-Practices-Outline-for-Years-1-4.pdf.

Index

For the benefit of digital users, indexed terms that span two pages (e.g., 52–53) may, on occasion, appear on only one of those pages.

Figures and boxes are indicated by *f* and *b* following the page number.